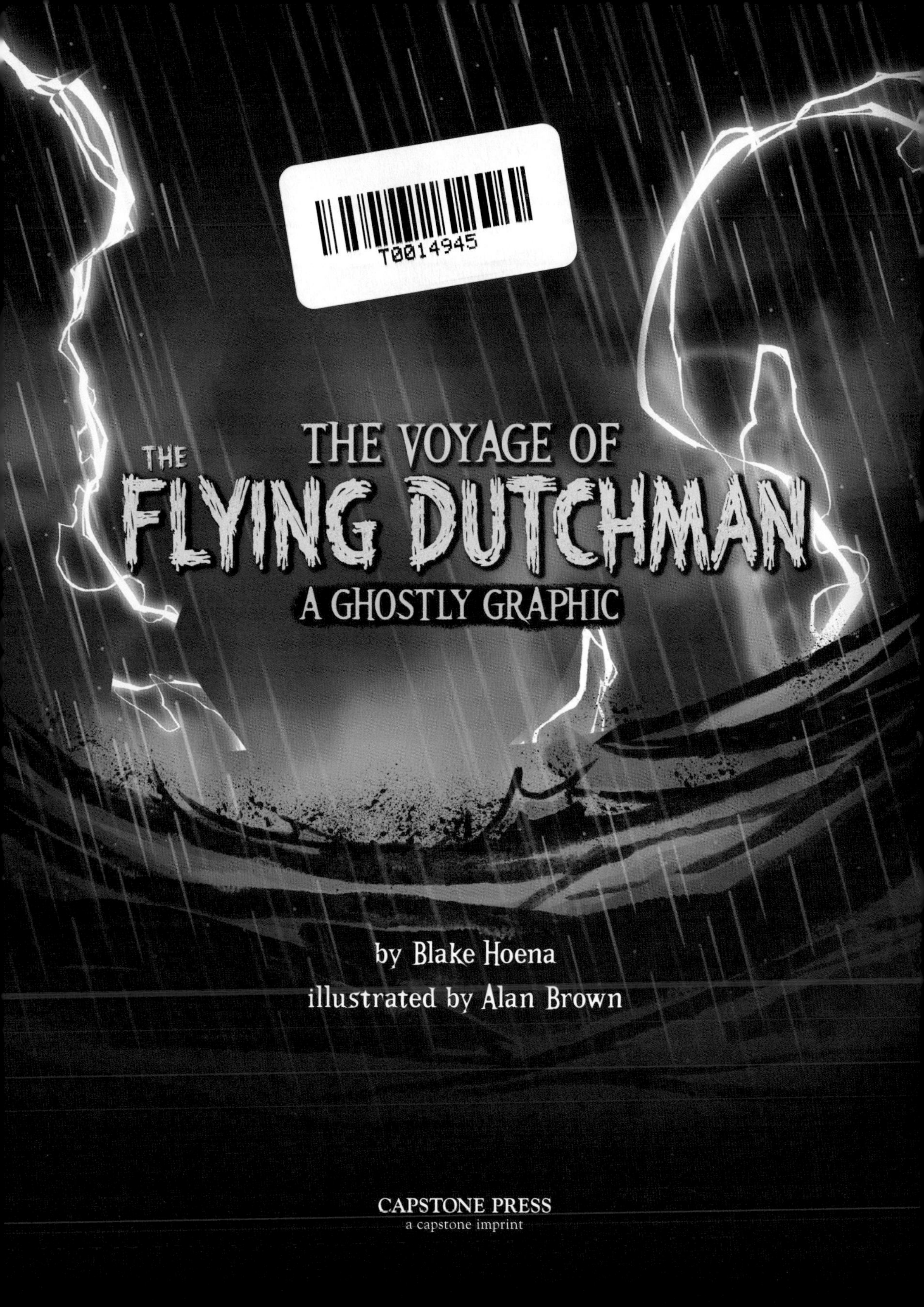

THE VOYAGE OF THE FLYING DUTCHMAN

A GHOSTLY GRAPHIC

by Blake Hoena
illustrated by Alan Brown

CAPSTONE PRESS
a capstone imprint

Published by Capstone Press, an imprint of Capstone
1710 Roe Crest Drive, North Mankato, Minnesota 56003
capstonepub.com

Library of Congress Cataloging-in-Publication Data
Names: Hoena, B. A., author. | Brown, Alan (Illustrator), illustrator.
Title: The voyage of the Flying Dutchman : a ghostly graphic / by Blake Hoena ;
illustrated by Alan Brown.
Description: North Mankato, Minnesota : Capstone Press, 2024. | Series: Ghostly
graphics | Includes bibliographical references. | Audience: Ages 9 to 11 | Audience:
Grades 4–6 | Summary: "For more than 400 years, the Flying Dutchman has
haunted the high seas. According to legend, the ghoulish ghost ship cannot
make port and must roam the waves forever. And should this sea specter be
sighted—beware! Spotting this vessel is believed to spell certain doom! Why must
the Flying Dutchman sail the seas for all eternity? And what frightening fates
have befallen those who have crossed its path? Young readers will find out in this
easy-to-read ghostly graphic novel that will send shivers down their spines!"
—Provided by publisher.
Identifiers: LCCN 2022047888 (print) | LCCN 2022047889 (ebook) |
ISBN 9781669050780 (hardcover) | ISBN 9781669071426 (paperback) |
ISBN 9781669050742 (pdf) | ISBN 9781669050766 (kindle edition) | ISBN
9781669050773 (epub)
Subjects: LCSH: Flying Dutchman—Comic books, strips, etc. |
LCGFT: Graphic novels
Classification: LCC GR75.F58 H64 2024 (print) | LCC GR75.F58 (ebook) | DDC
398.25—dc23/eng/20221213
LC record available at https://lccn.loc.gov/2022047888
LC ebook record available at https://lccn.loc.gov/2022047889

Editorial Credits
Editor: Christopher Harbo; Designer: Sarah Bennett;
Production Specialist: Katy LaVigne

Printed in the United States   5731

TABLE OF CONTENTS

CHAPTER 1
SAILING INTO THE STORM

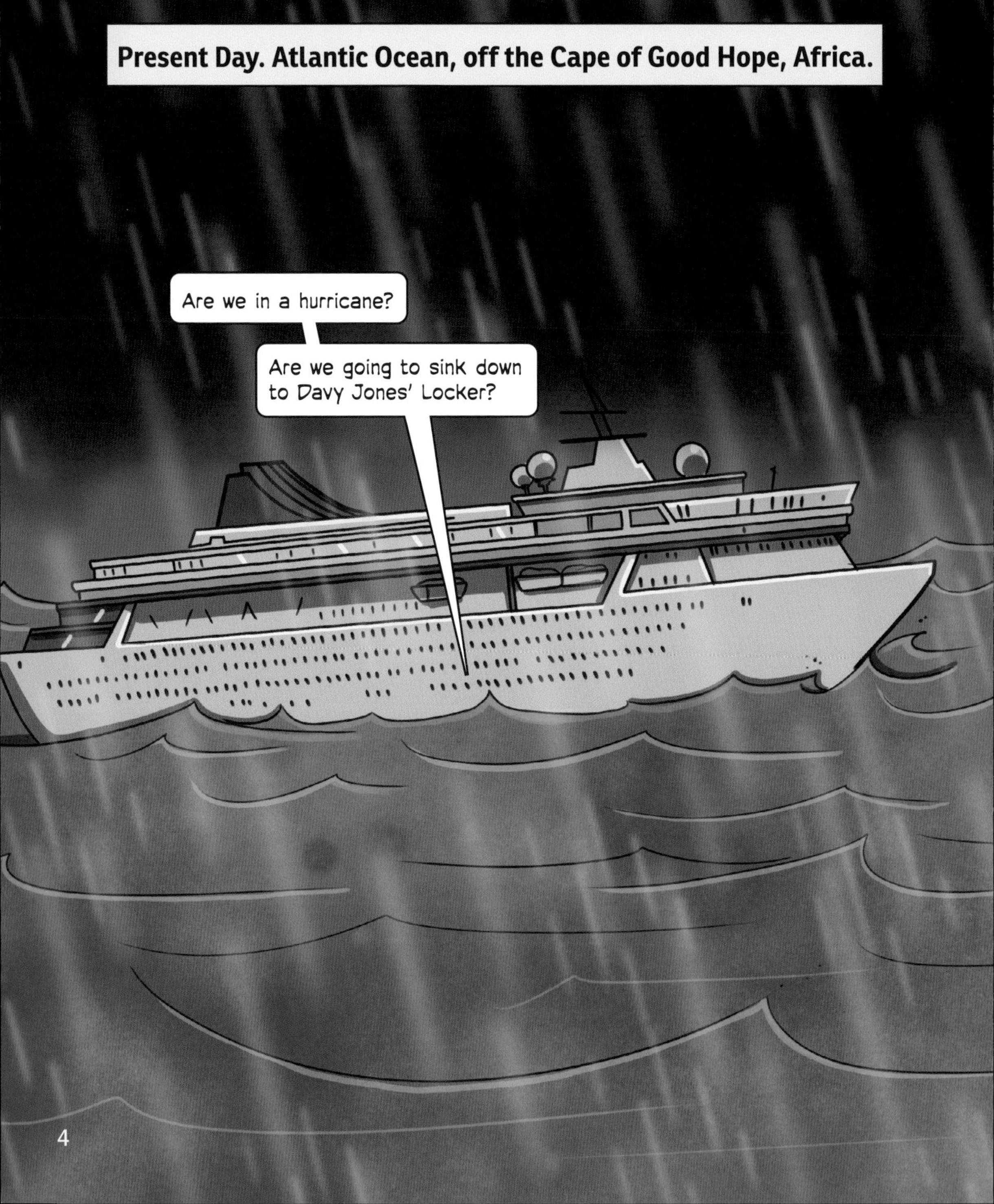
Present Day. Atlantic Ocean, off the Cape of Good Hope, Africa.
Are we in a hurricane?
Are we going to sink down to Davy Jones' Locker?

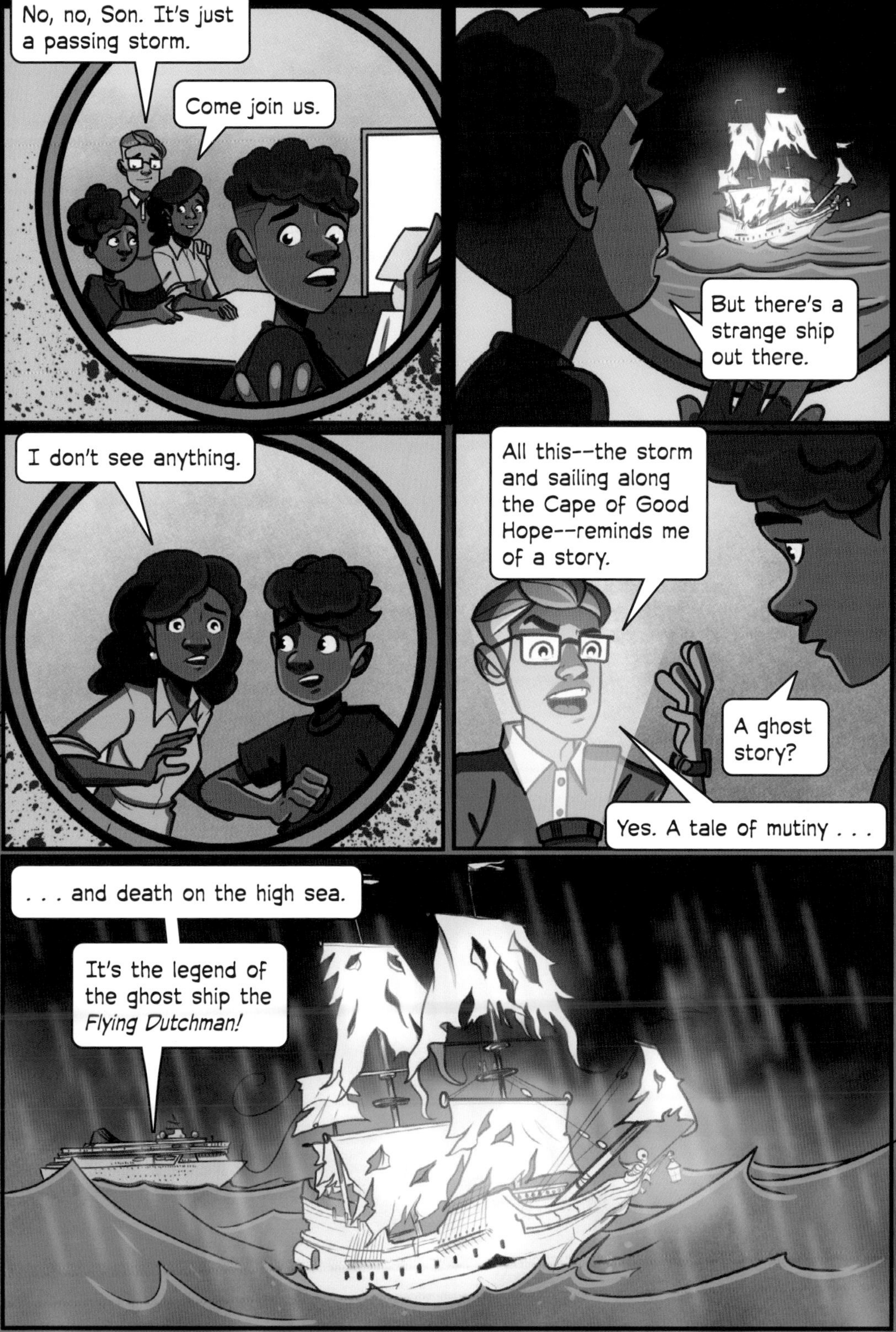
No, no, Son. It's just a passing storm.
Come join us.
But there's a strange ship out there.
I don't see anything.
All this--the storm and sailing along the Cape of Good Hope--reminds me of a story.
A ghost story?
Yes. A tale of mutiny . . .
. . . and death on the high sea.
It's the legend of the ghost ship the *Flying Dutchman!*

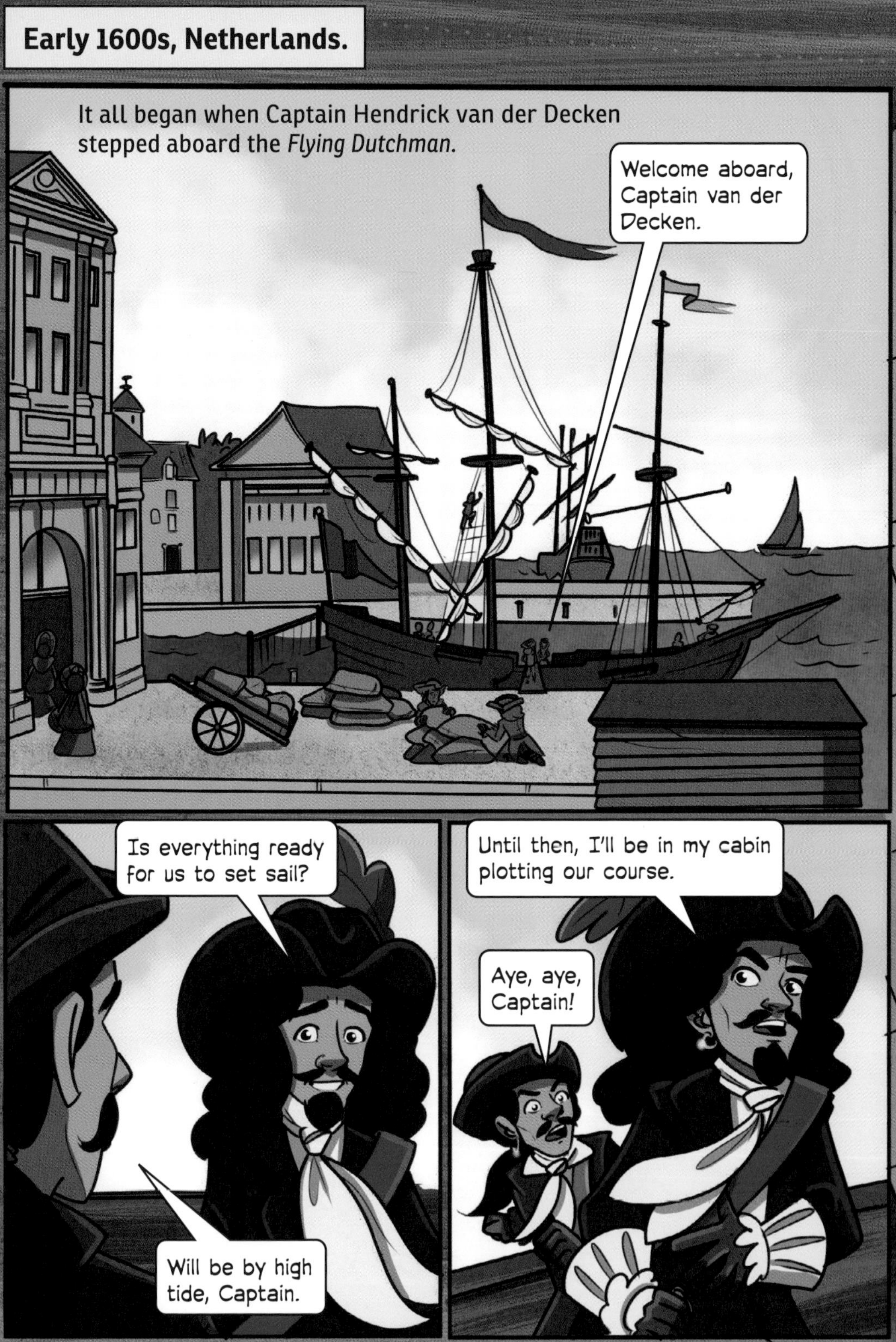
Early 1600s, Netherlands.
It all began when Captain Hendrick van der Decken stepped aboard the *Flying Dutchman*.
Welcome aboard, Captain van der Decken.
Is everything ready for us to set sail?
Will be by high tide, Captain.
Until then, I'll be in my cabin plotting our course.
Aye, aye, Captain!

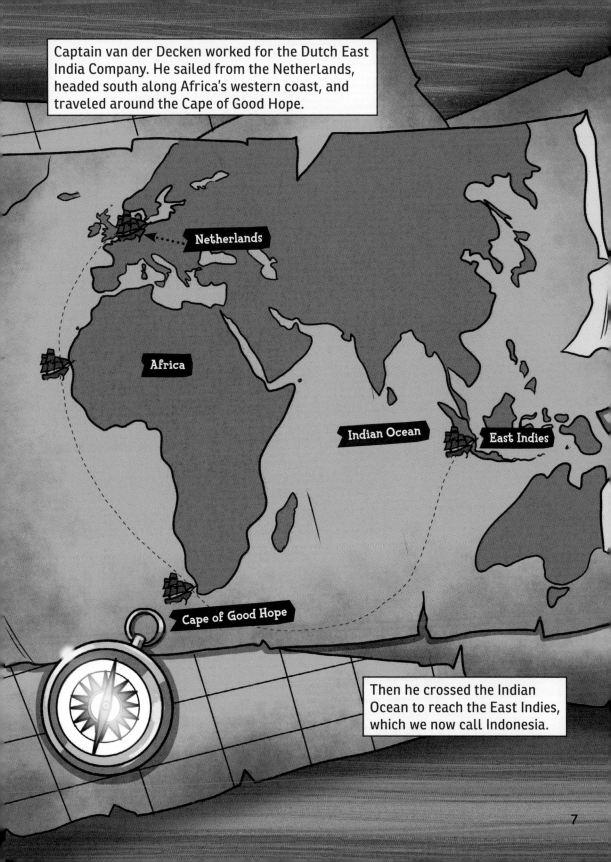

Captain van der Decken worked for the Dutch East India Company. He sailed from the Netherlands, headed south along Africa's western coast, and traveled around the Cape of Good Hope.

Netherlands

Africa

Indian Ocean

East Indies

Cape of Good Hope

Then he crossed the Indian Ocean to reach the East Indies, which we now call Indonesia.

The journey there was uneventful. The *Flying Dutchman* was loaded up with spices that would be sold back in Europe.

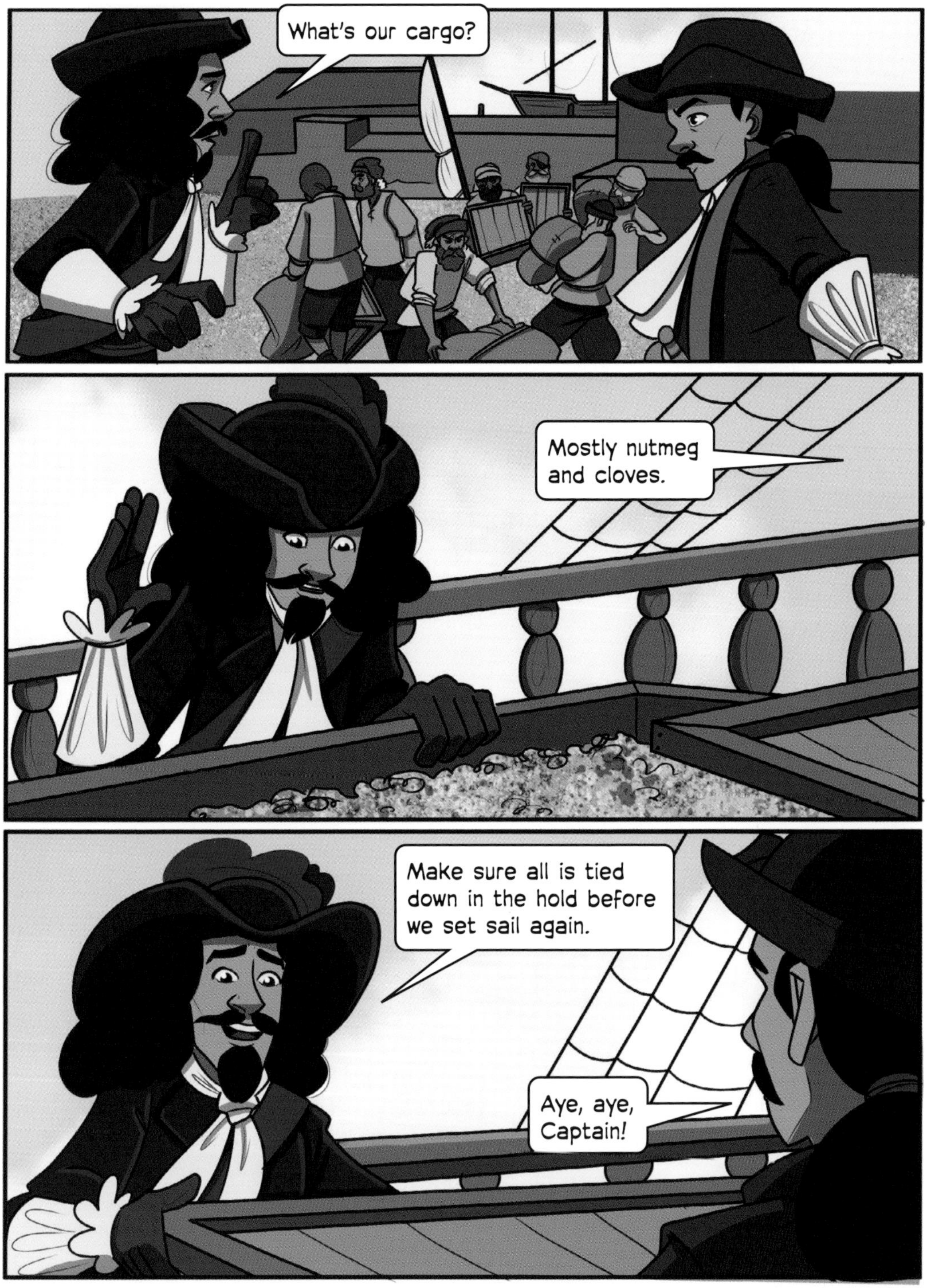
What's our cargo?
Mostly nutmeg and cloves.
Make sure all is tied down in the hold before we set sail again.
Aye, aye, Captain!

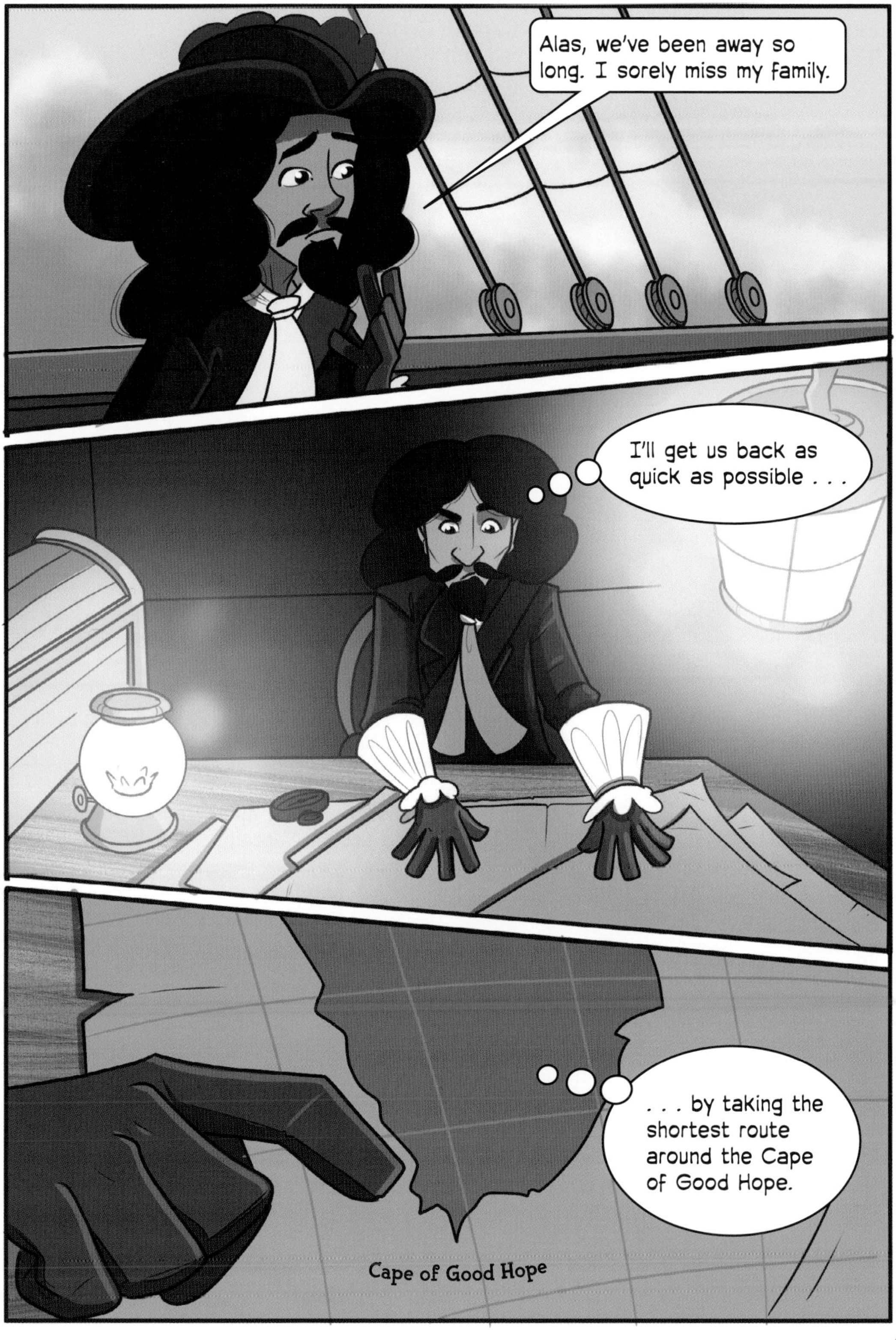
Alas, we've been away so long. I sorely miss my family.
I'll get us back as quick as possible . . .
. . . by taking the shortest route around the Cape of Good Hope.
Cape of Good Hope

Explorers had a nickname for the Cape of Good Hope.
They called it the Cape of Storms.

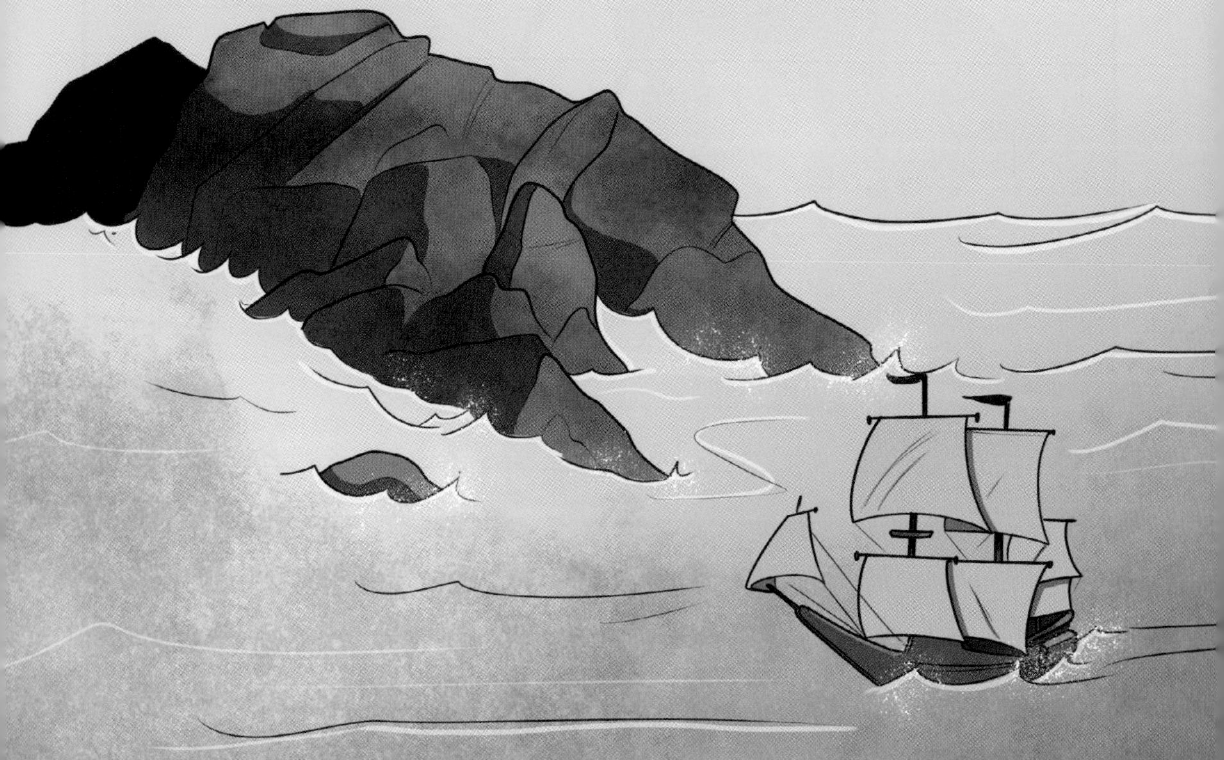

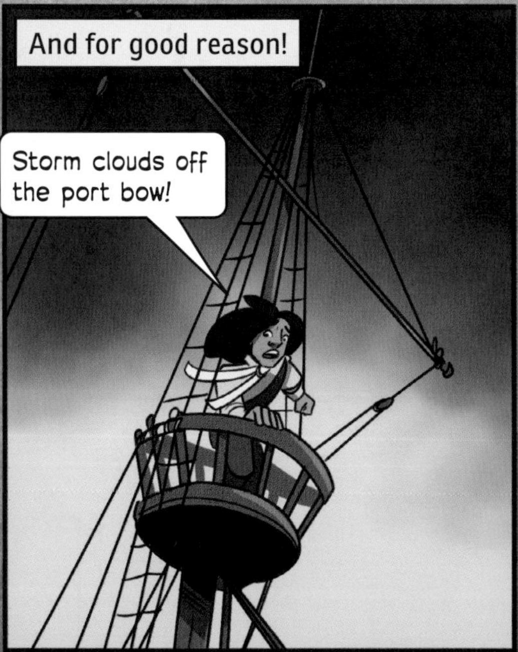
And for good reason!
Storm clouds off the port bow!

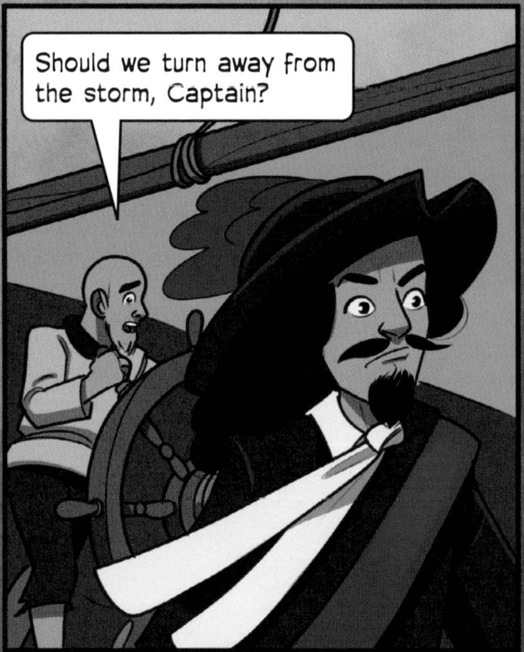
Should we turn away from the storm, Captain?

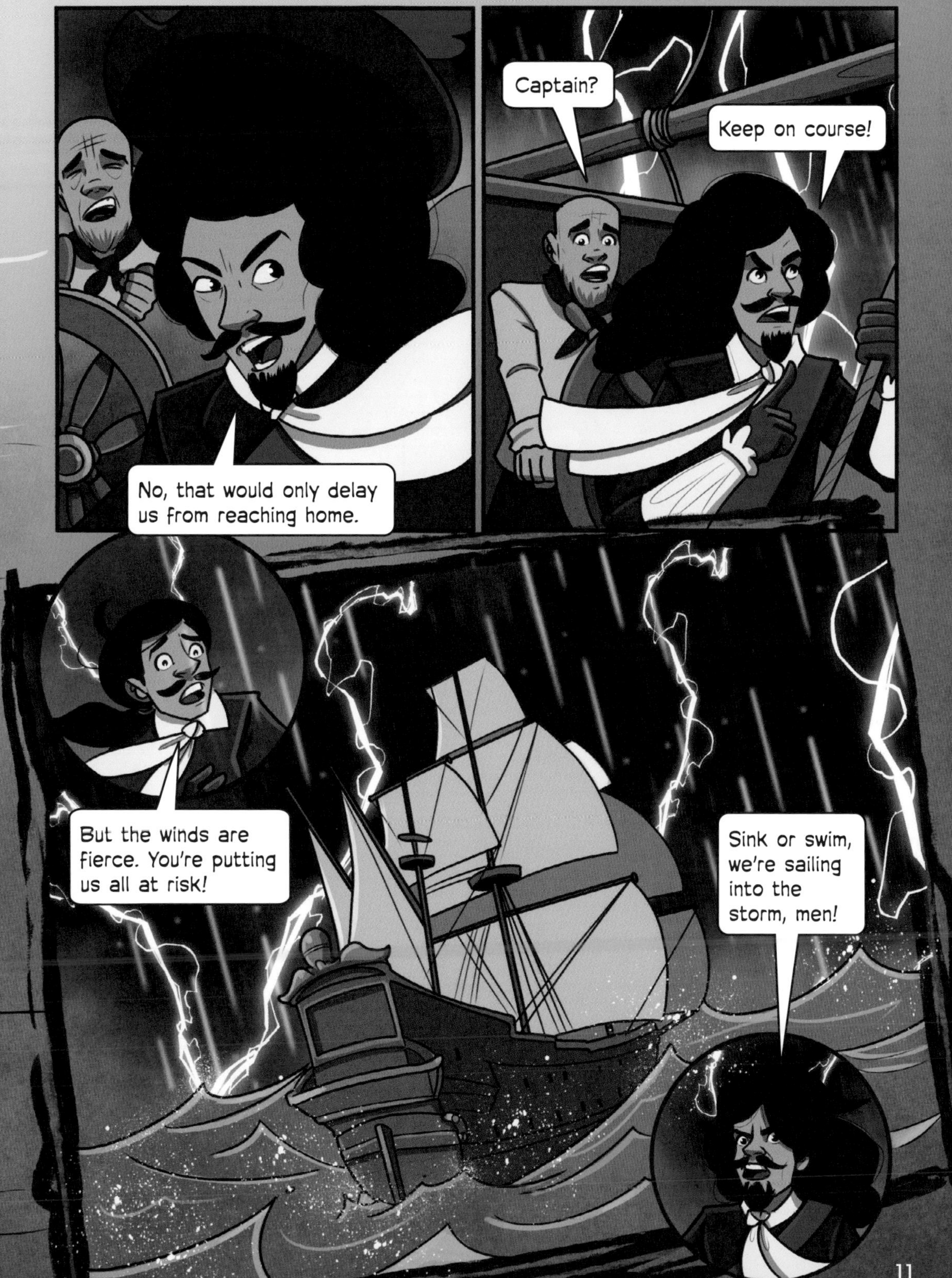
No, that would only delay us from reaching home.
Captain?
Keep on course!
But the winds are fierce. You're putting us all at risk!
Sink or swim, we're sailing into the storm, men!

CHAPTER 2

DEAL WITH THE DEVIL

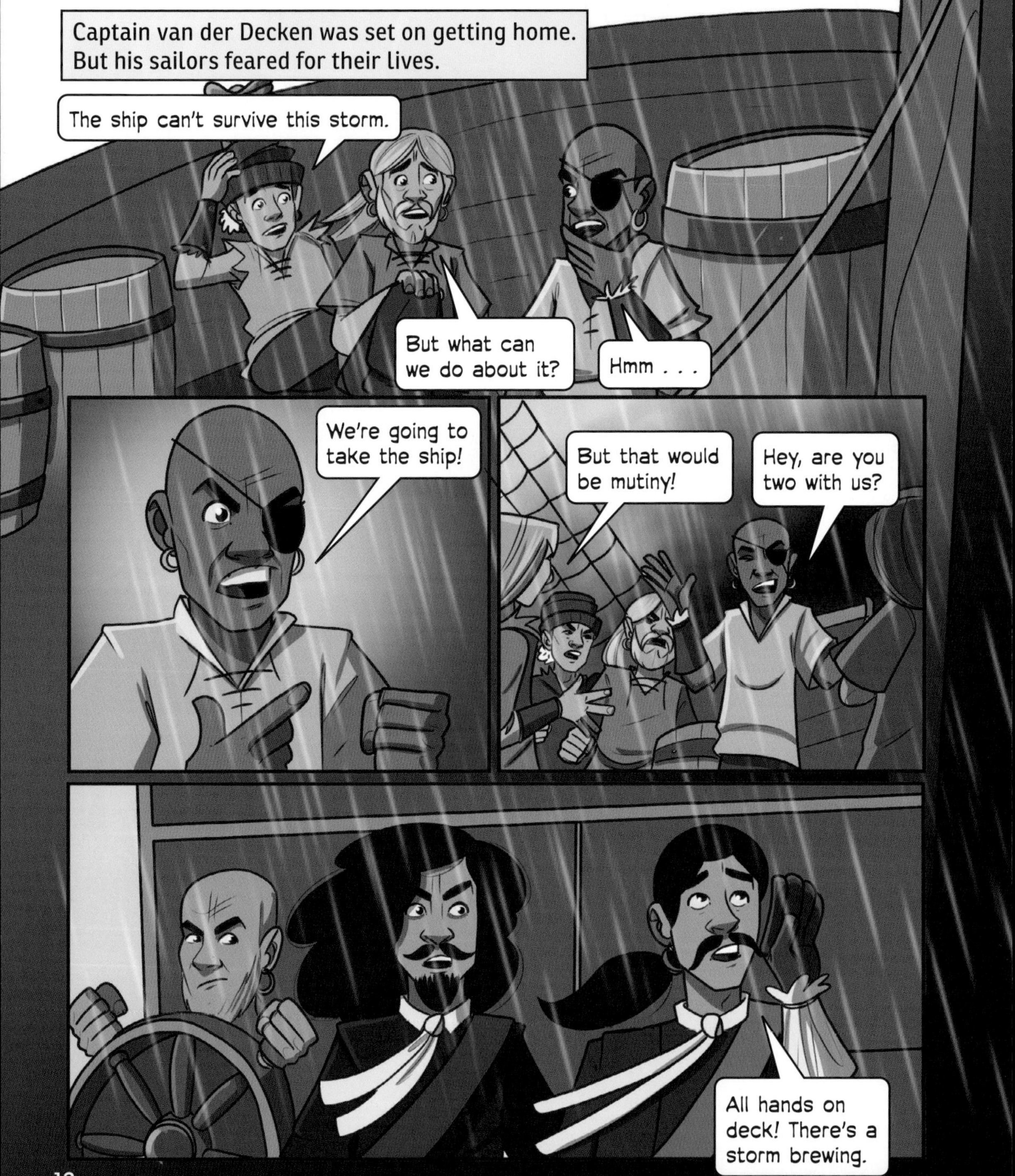

Captain van der Decken was set on getting home. But his sailors feared for their lives.
The ship can't survive this storm.
But what can we do about it?
Hmm . . .
We're going to take the ship!
But that would be mutiny!
Hey, are you two with us?
All hands on deck! There's a storm brewing.

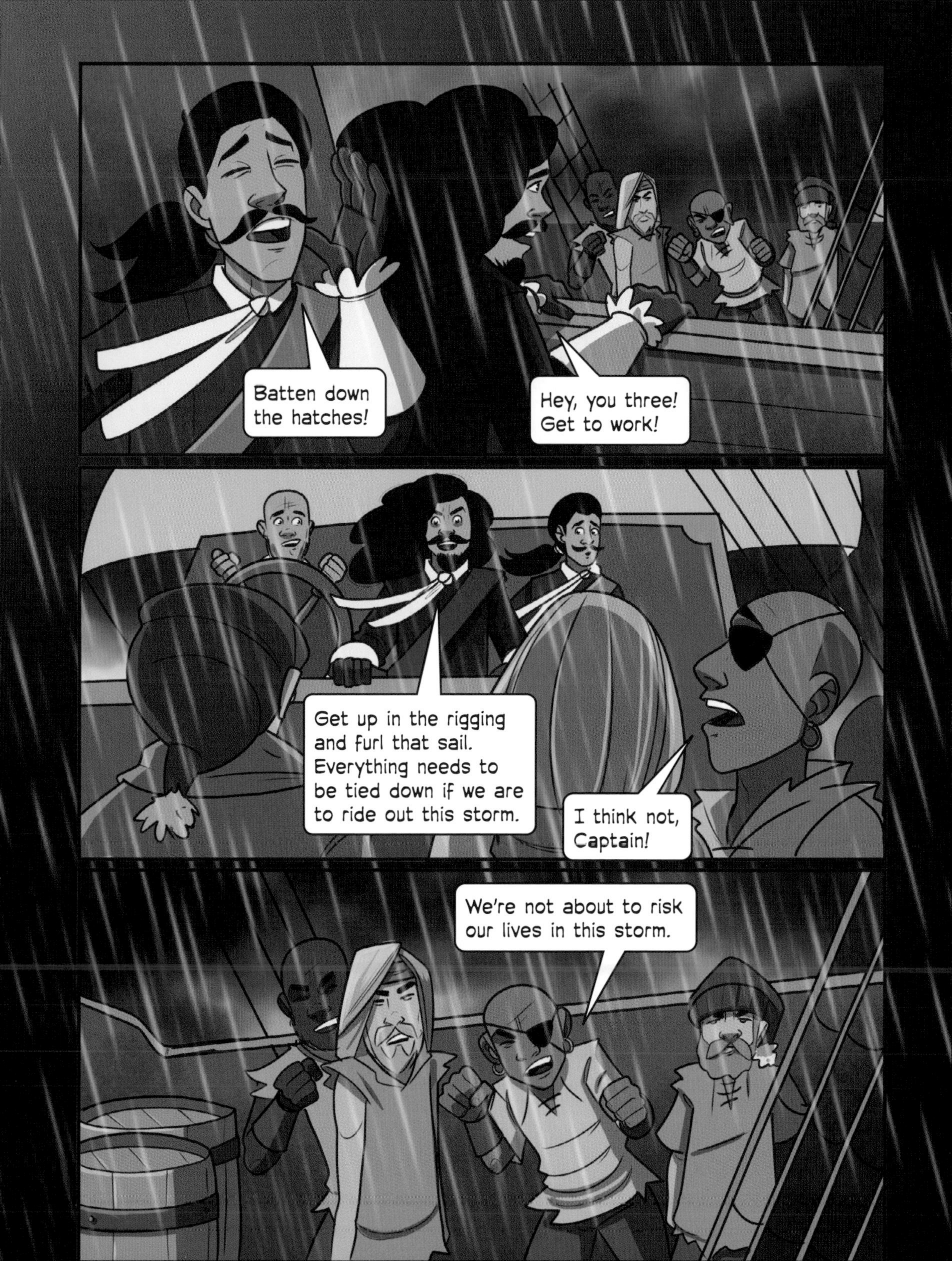
Batten down the hatches!
Hey, you three! Get to work!
Get up in the rigging and furl that sail. Everything needs to be tied down if we are to ride out this storm.
I think not, Captain!
We're not about to risk our lives in this storm.

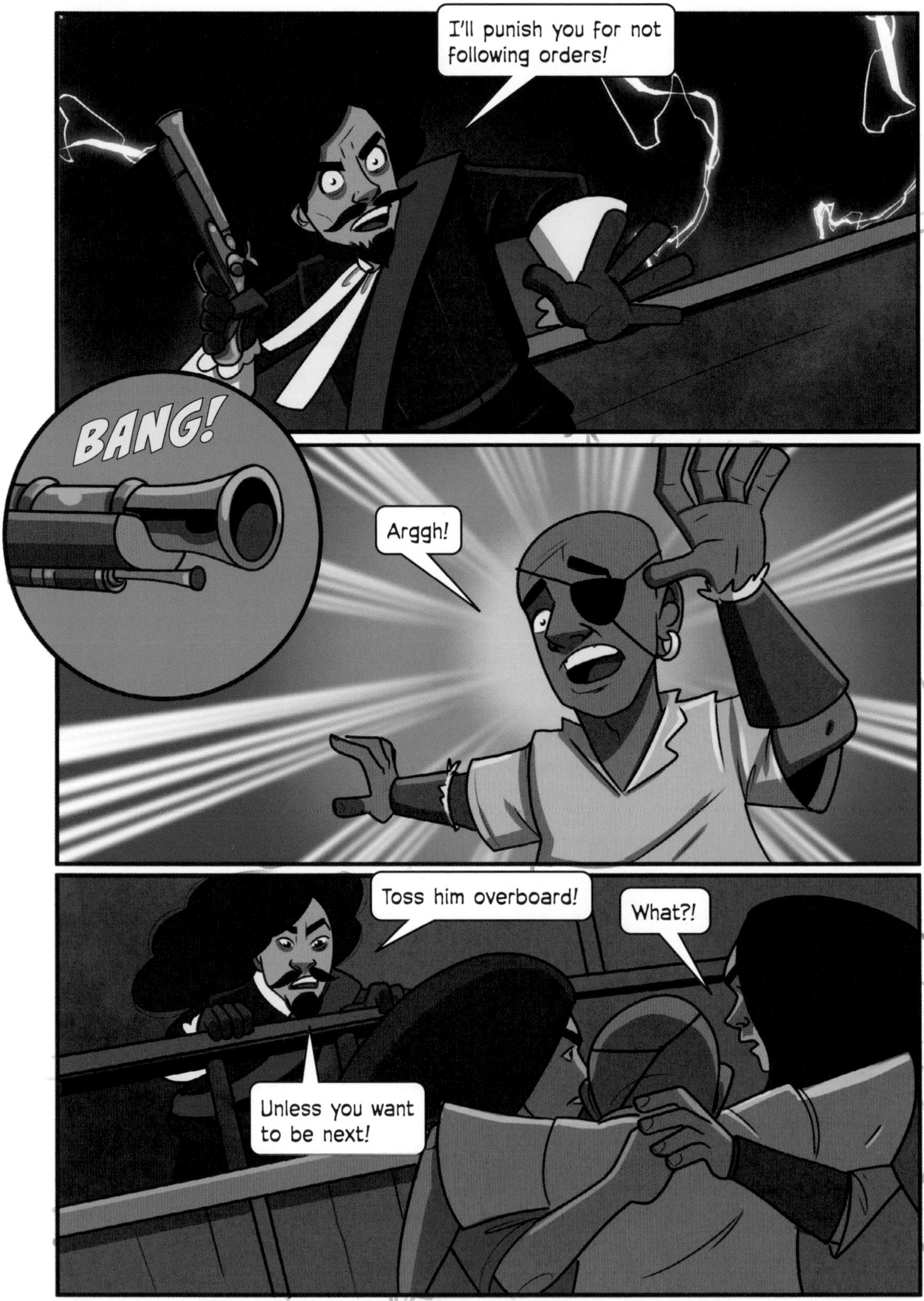
I'll punish you for not following orders!
BANG!
Arggh!
Toss him overboard!
What?!
Unless you want to be next!

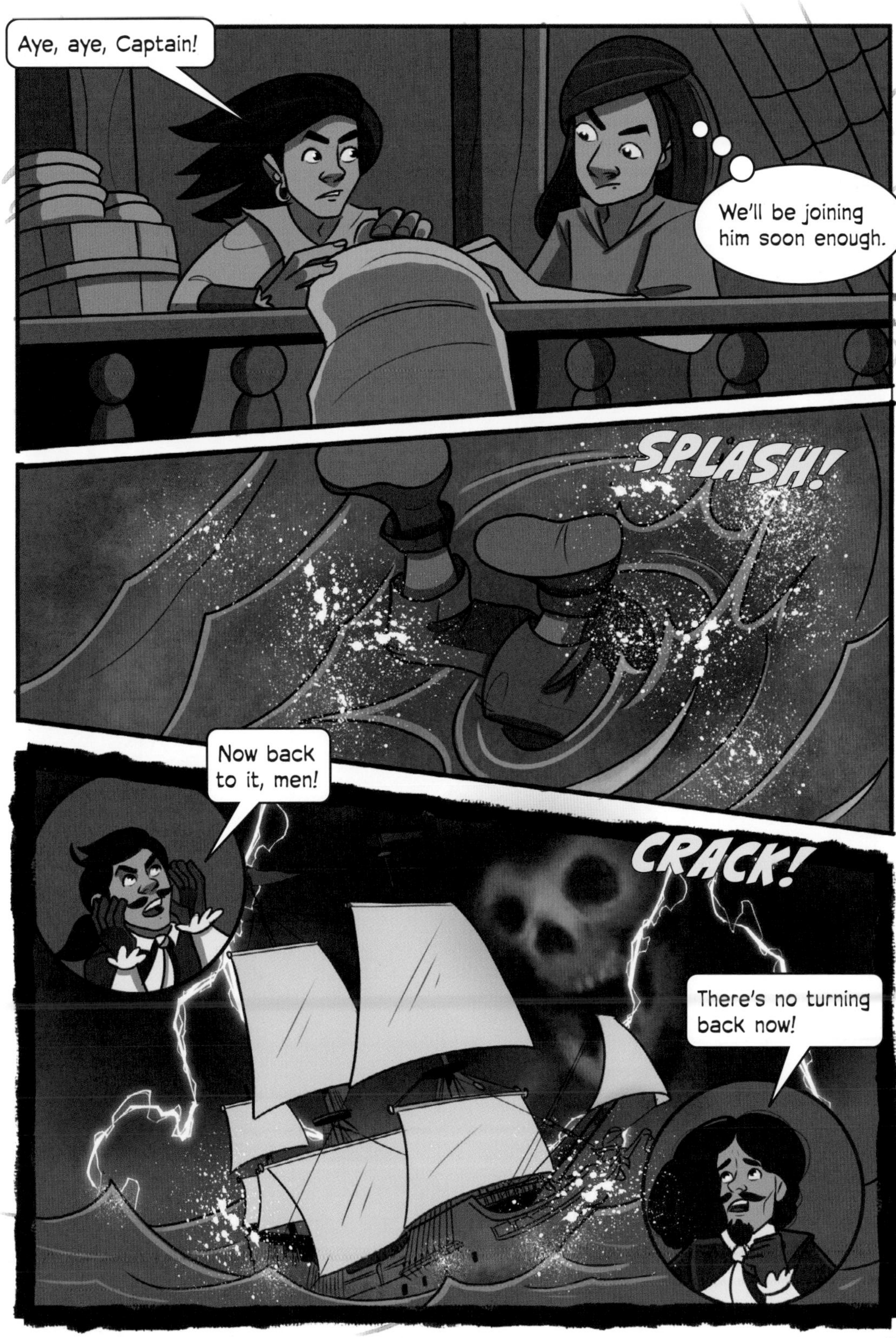
Aye, aye, Captain!
We'll be joining him soon enough.
SPLASH!
Now back to it, men!
CRACK!
There's no turning back now!

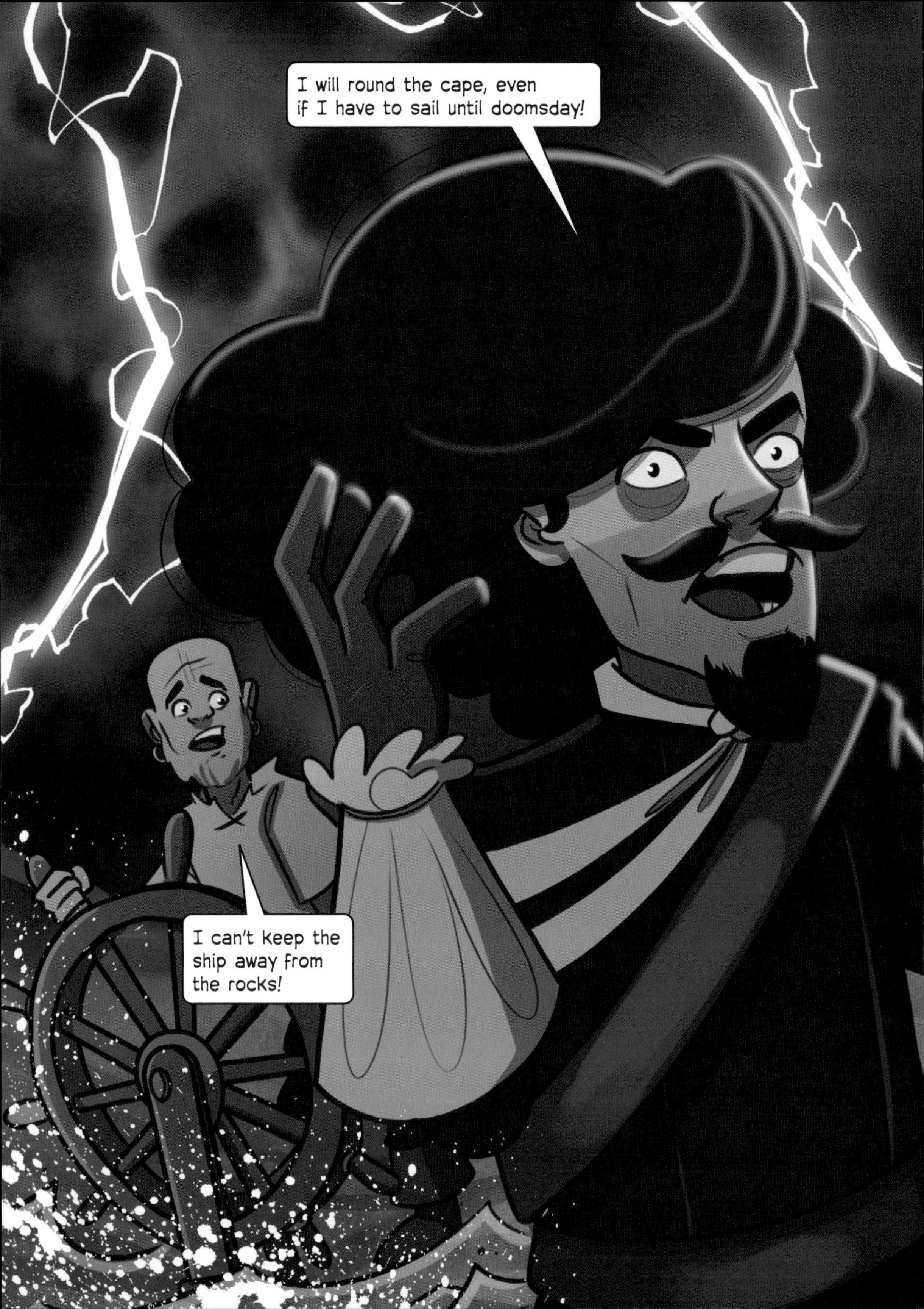
I will round the cape, even if I have to sail until doomsday!
I can't keep the ship away from the rocks!

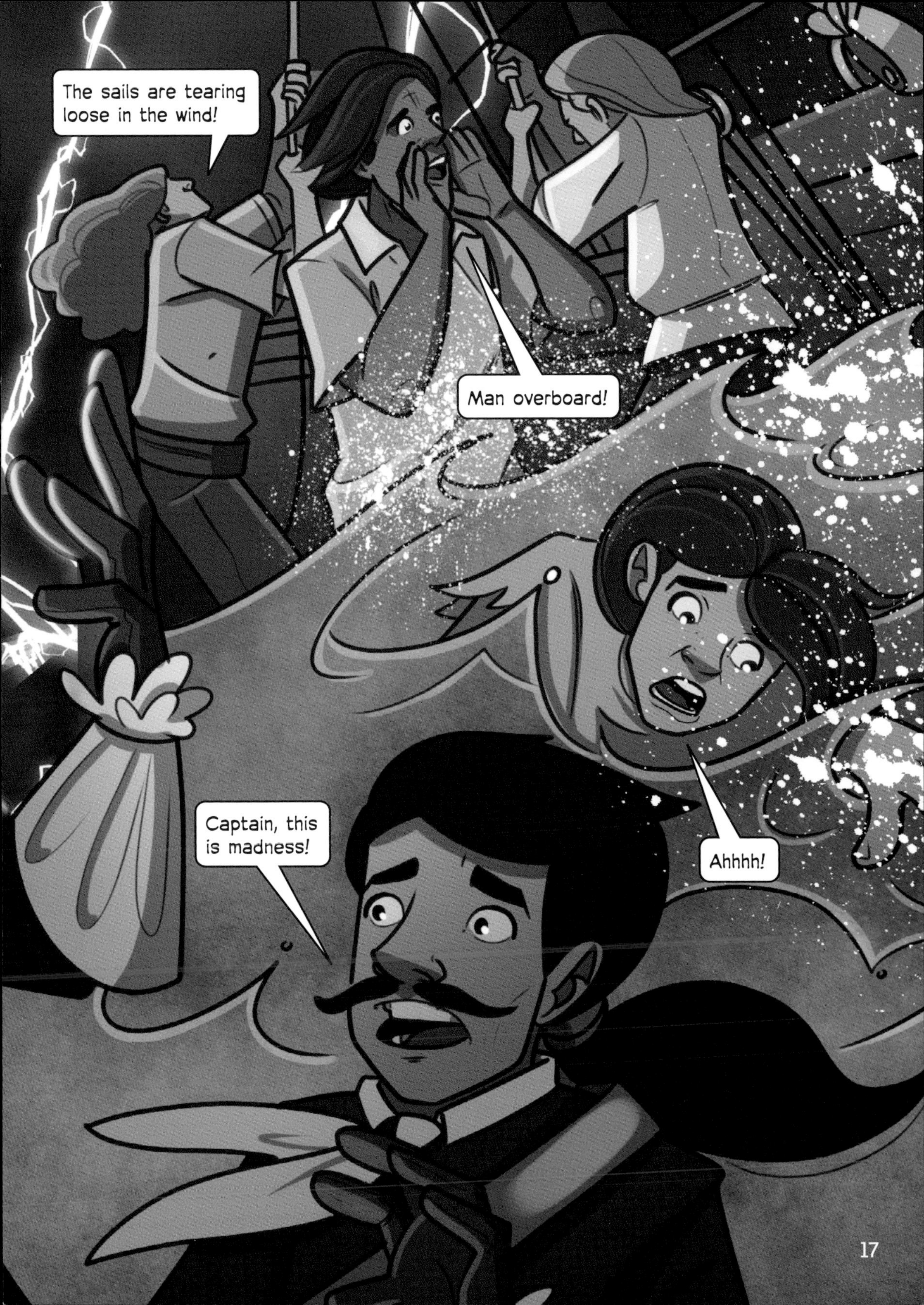
The sails are tearing loose in the wind!
Man overboard!
Ahhhh!
Captain, this is madness!

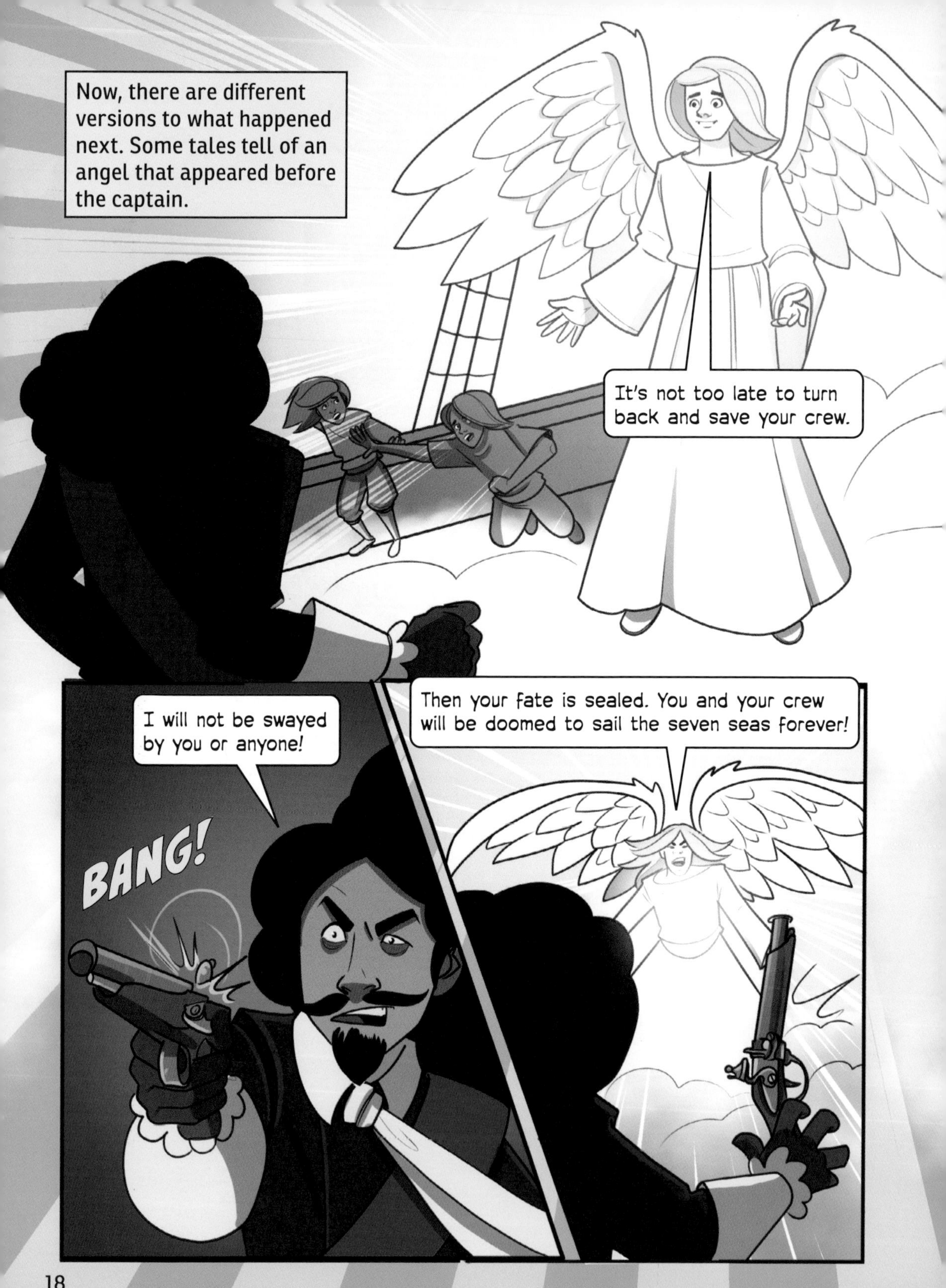
Now, there are different versions to what happened next. Some tales tell of an angel that appeared before the captain.
It's not too late to turn back and save your crew.
I will not be swayed by you or anyone!
BANG!
Then your fate is sealed. You and your crew will be doomed to sail the seven seas forever!

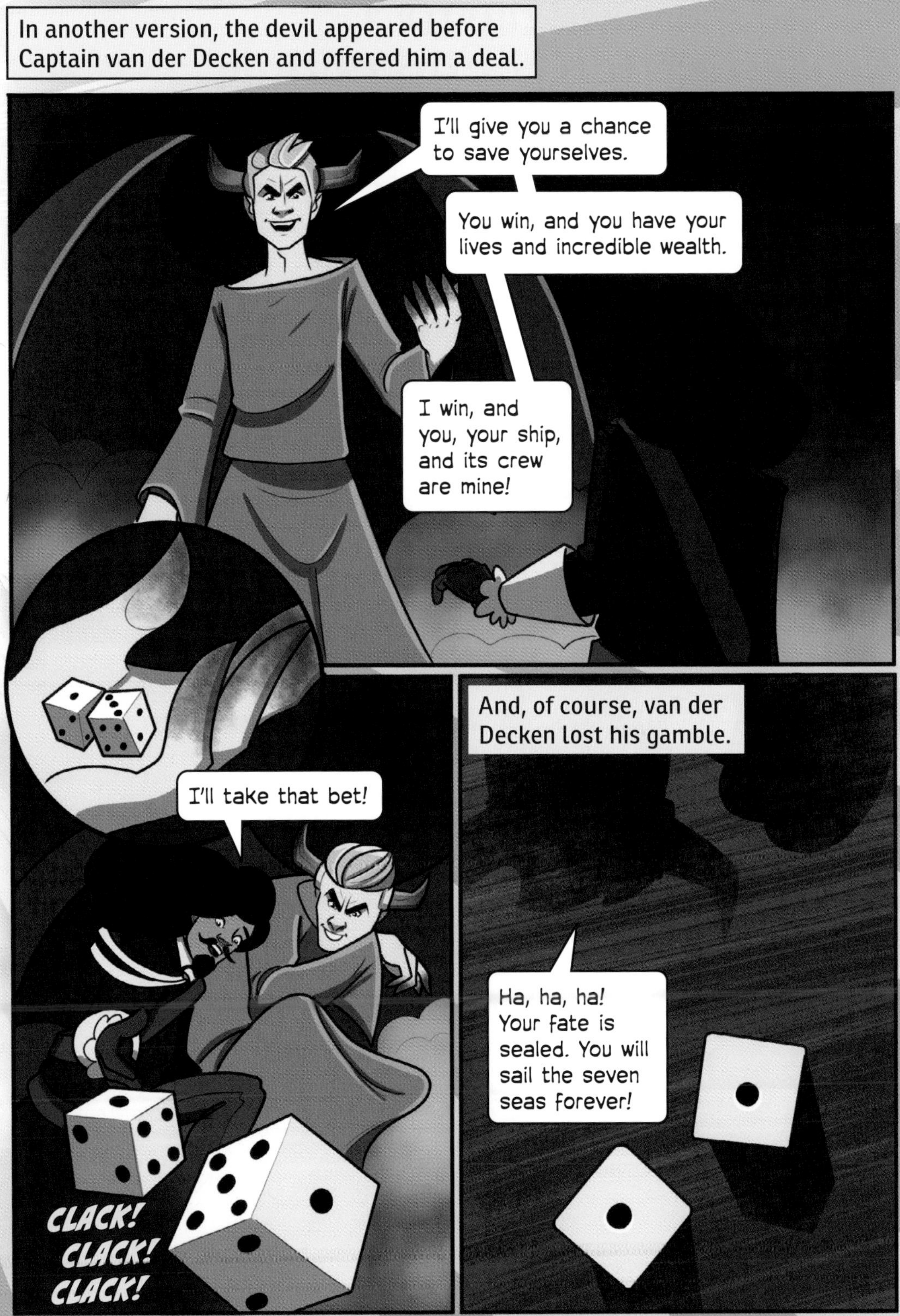
In another version, the devil appeared before Captain van der Decken and offered him a deal.
I'll give you a chance to save yourselves.
You win, and you have your lives and incredible wealth.
I win, and you, your ship, and its crew are mine!
I'll take that bet!
CLACK! CLACK! CLACK!
And, of course, van der Decken lost his gamble.
Ha, ha, ha! Your fate is sealed. You will sail the seven seas forever!

CHAPTER 3
THE LEGEND GROWS

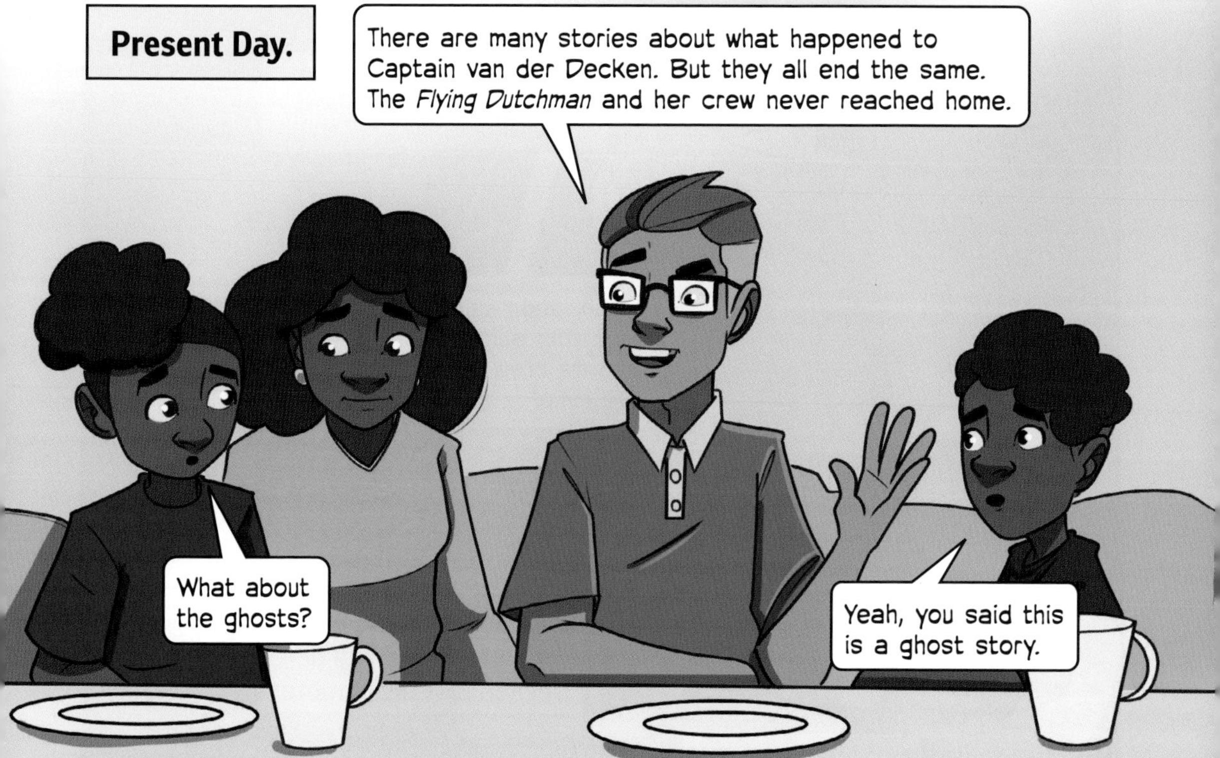
Present Day.
There are many stories about what happened to Captain van der Decken. But they all end the same. The *Flying Dutchman* and her crew never reached home.
What about the ghosts?
Yeah, you said this is a ghost story.

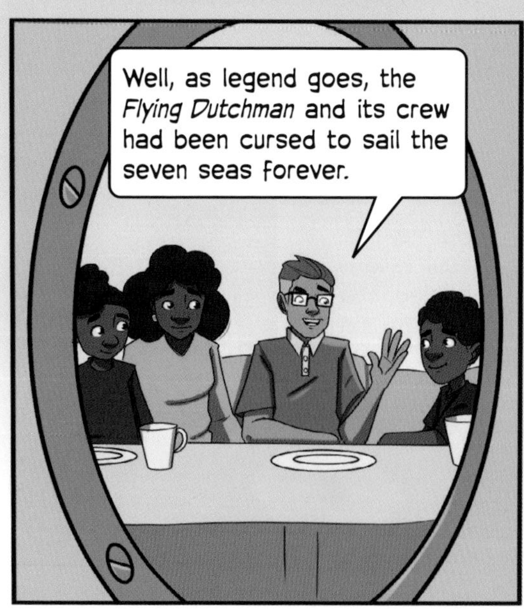
Well, as legend goes, the *Flying Dutchman* and its crew had been cursed to sail the seven seas forever.

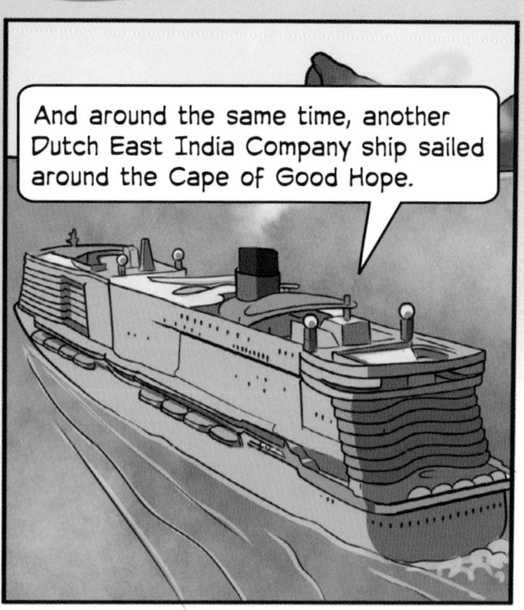
And around the same time, another Dutch East India Company ship sailed around the Cape of Good Hope.

Mid-1600s, Netherlands.

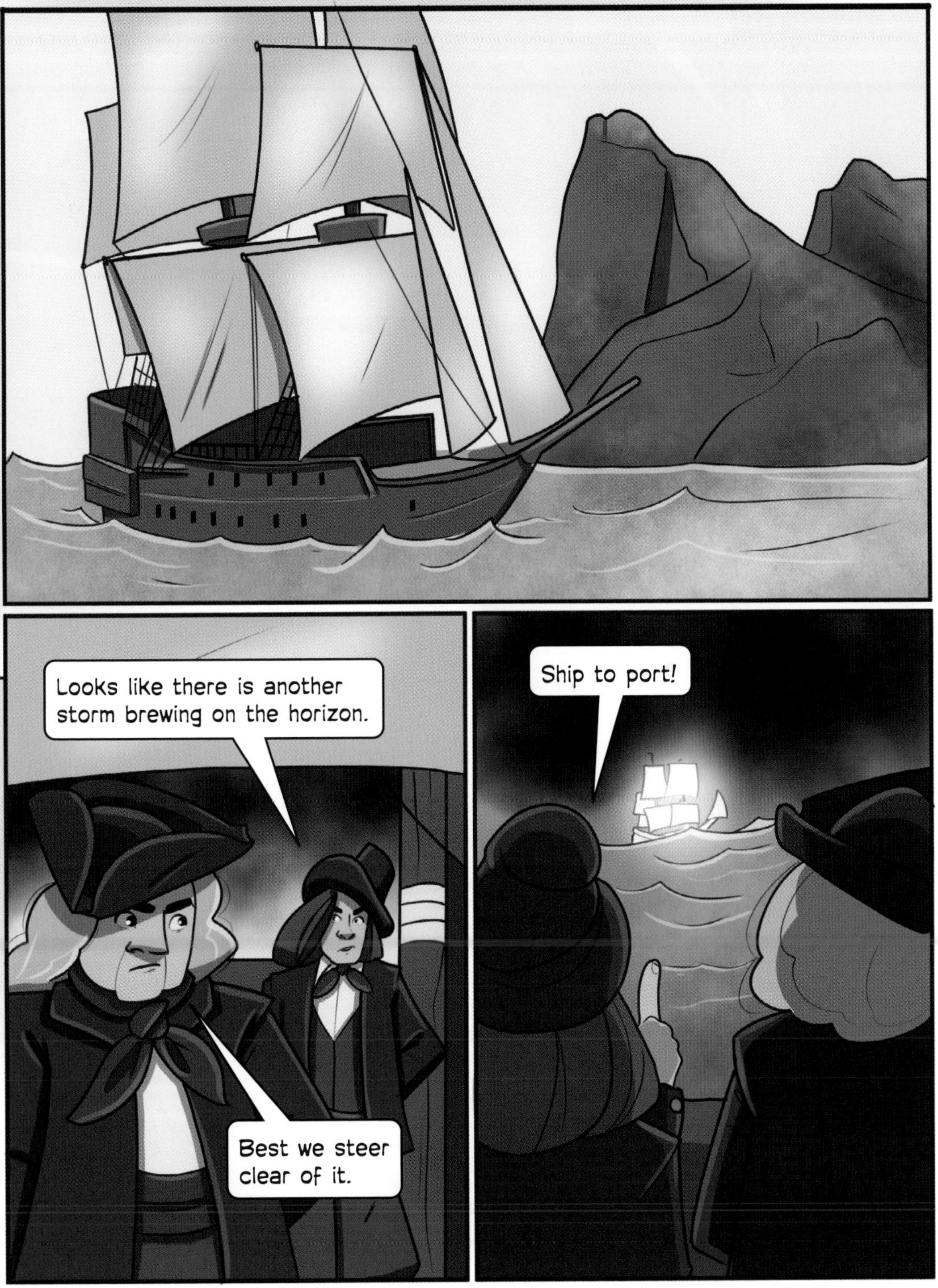
Looks like there is another storm brewing on the horizon.
Best we steer clear of it.
Ship to port!

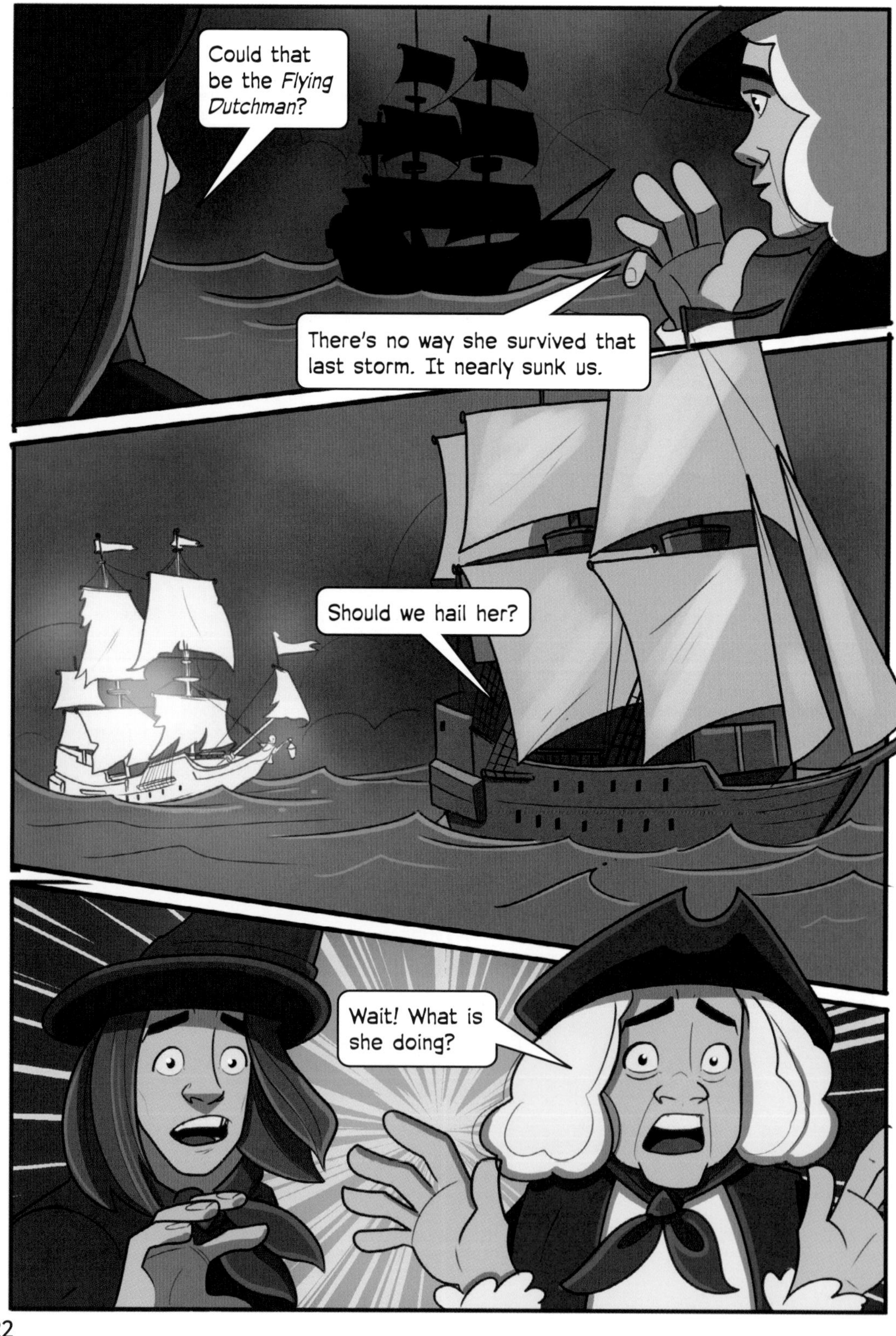
Could that be the *Flying Dutchman*?
There's no way she survived that last storm. It nearly sunk us.
Should we hail her?
Wait! What is she doing?

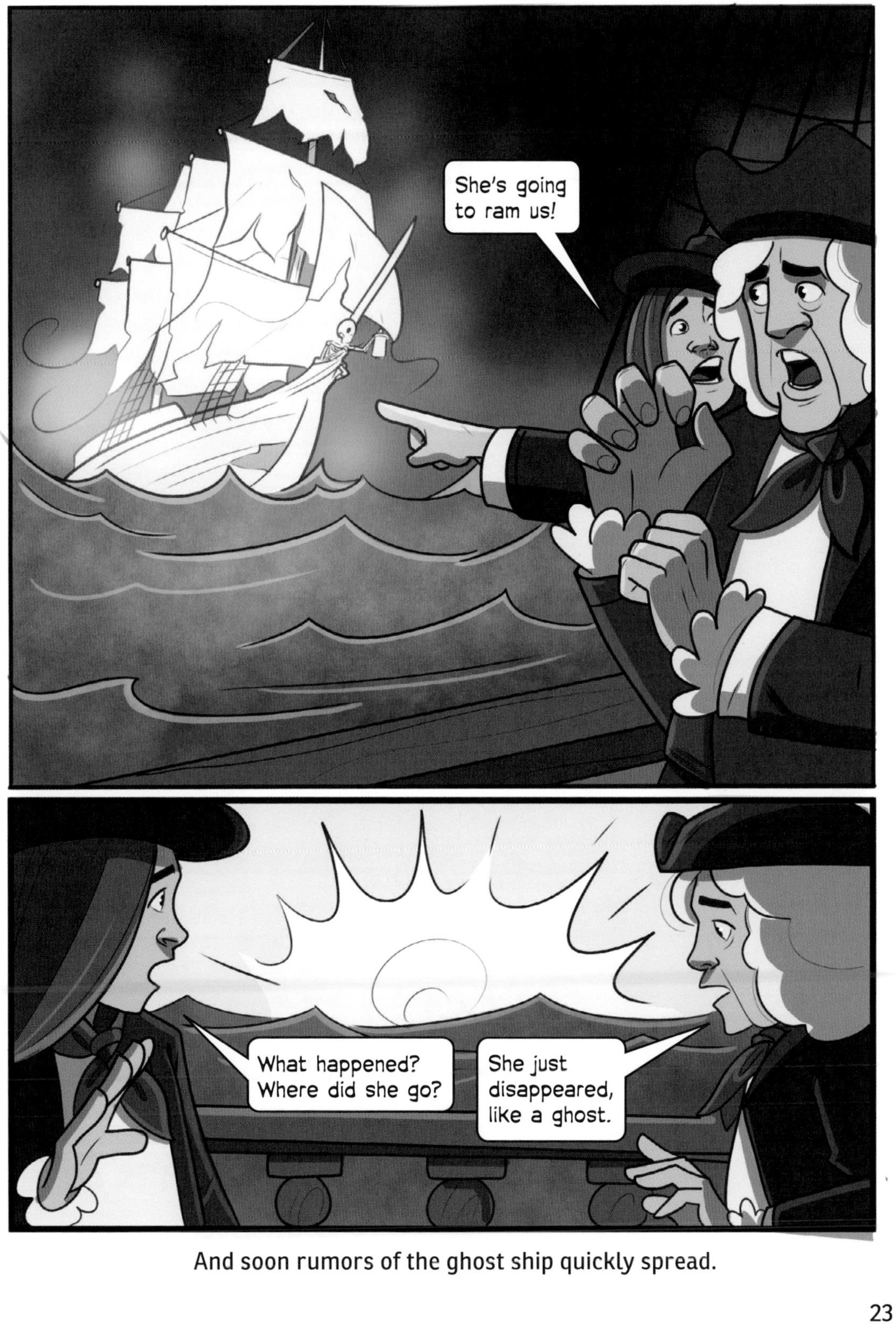
She's going to ram us!
What happened? Where did she go?
She just disappeared, like a ghost.

And soon rumors of the ghost ship quickly spread.

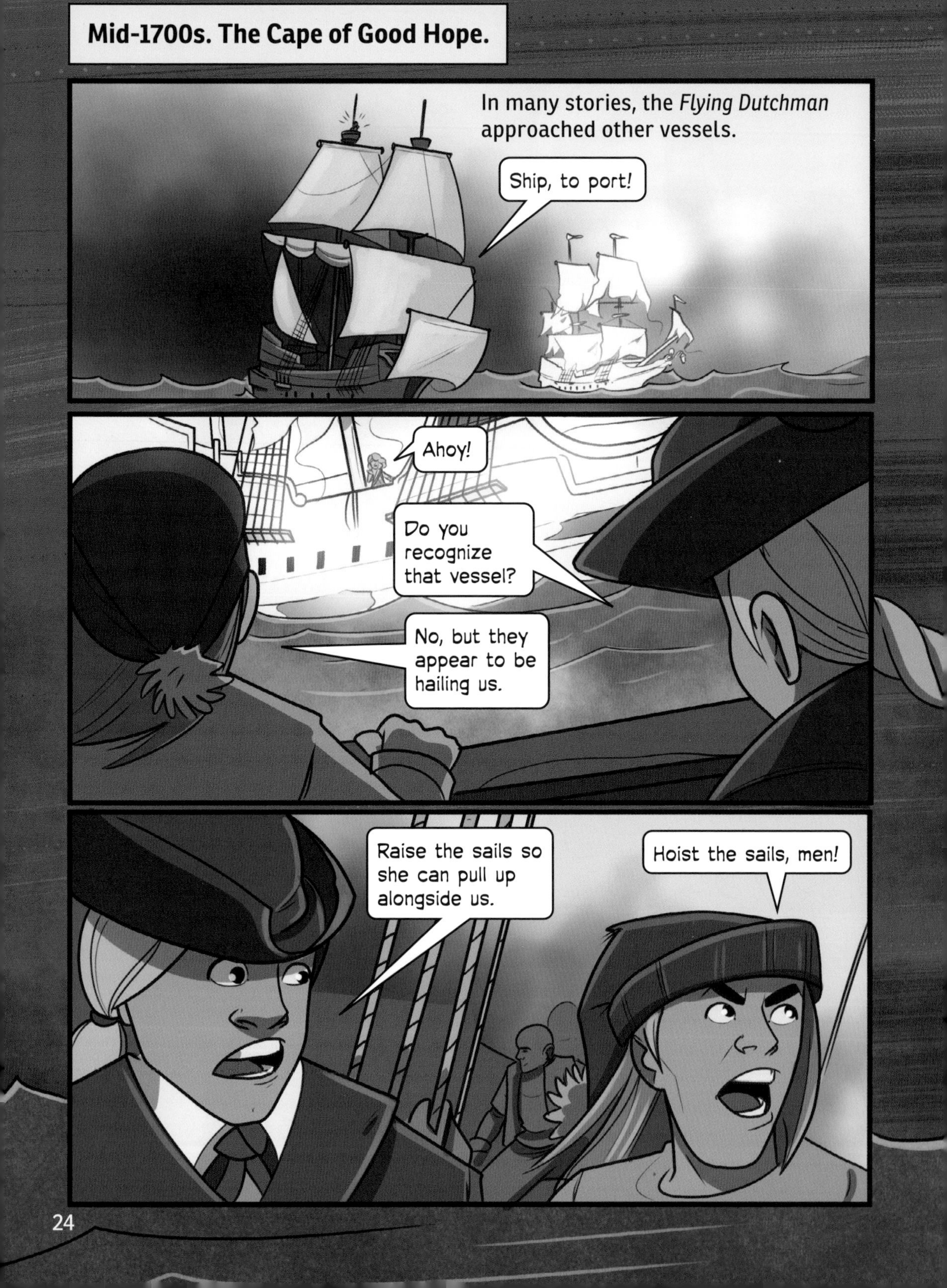
Mid-1700s. The Cape of Good Hope.
In many stories, the *Flying Dutchman* approached other vessels.
Ship, to port!
Ahoy!
Do you recognize that vessel?
No, but they appear to be hailing us.
Raise the sails so she can pull up alongside us.
Hoist the sails, men!

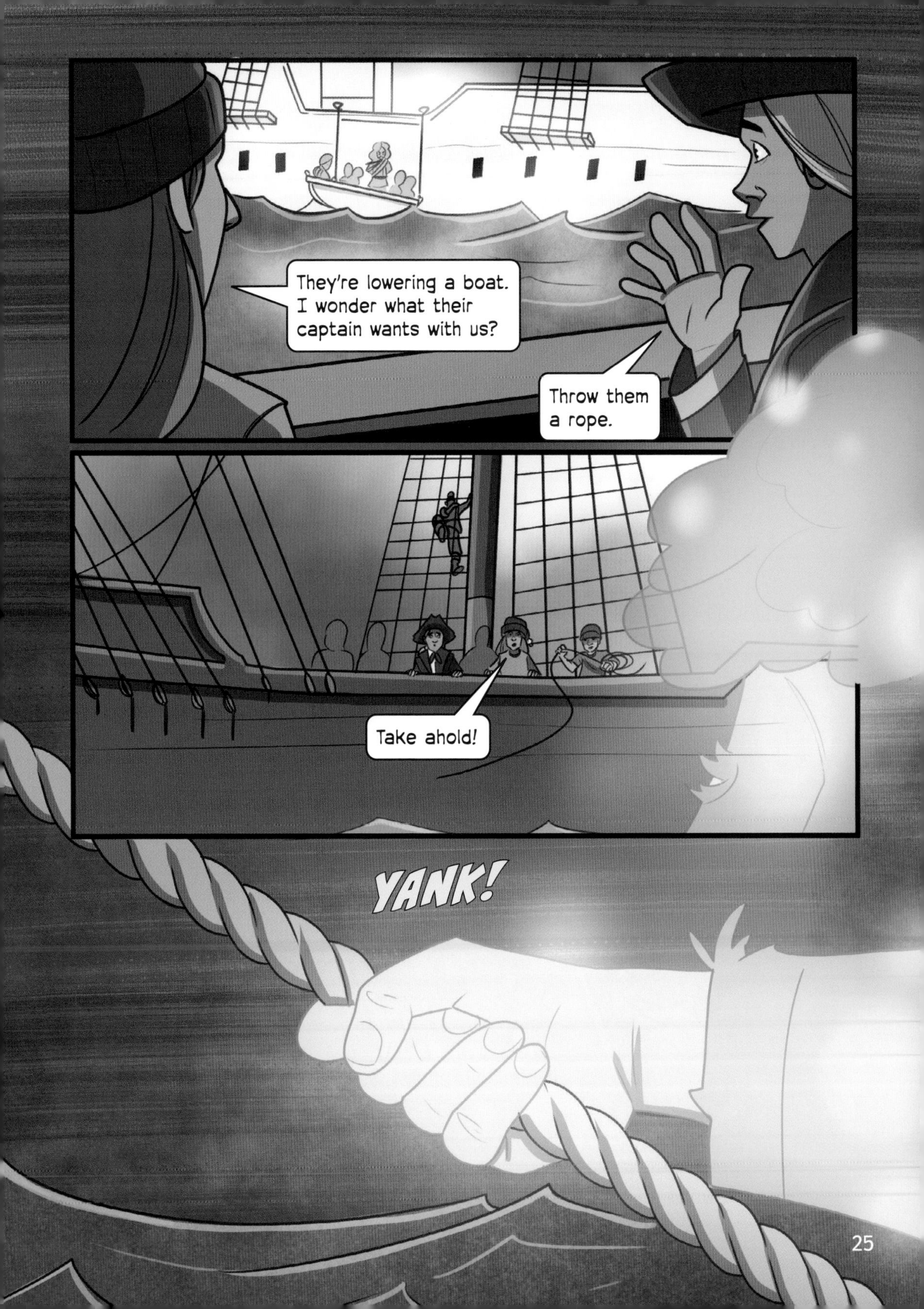
They're lowering a boat. I wonder what their captain wants with us?
Throw them a rope.
Take ahold!
YANK!

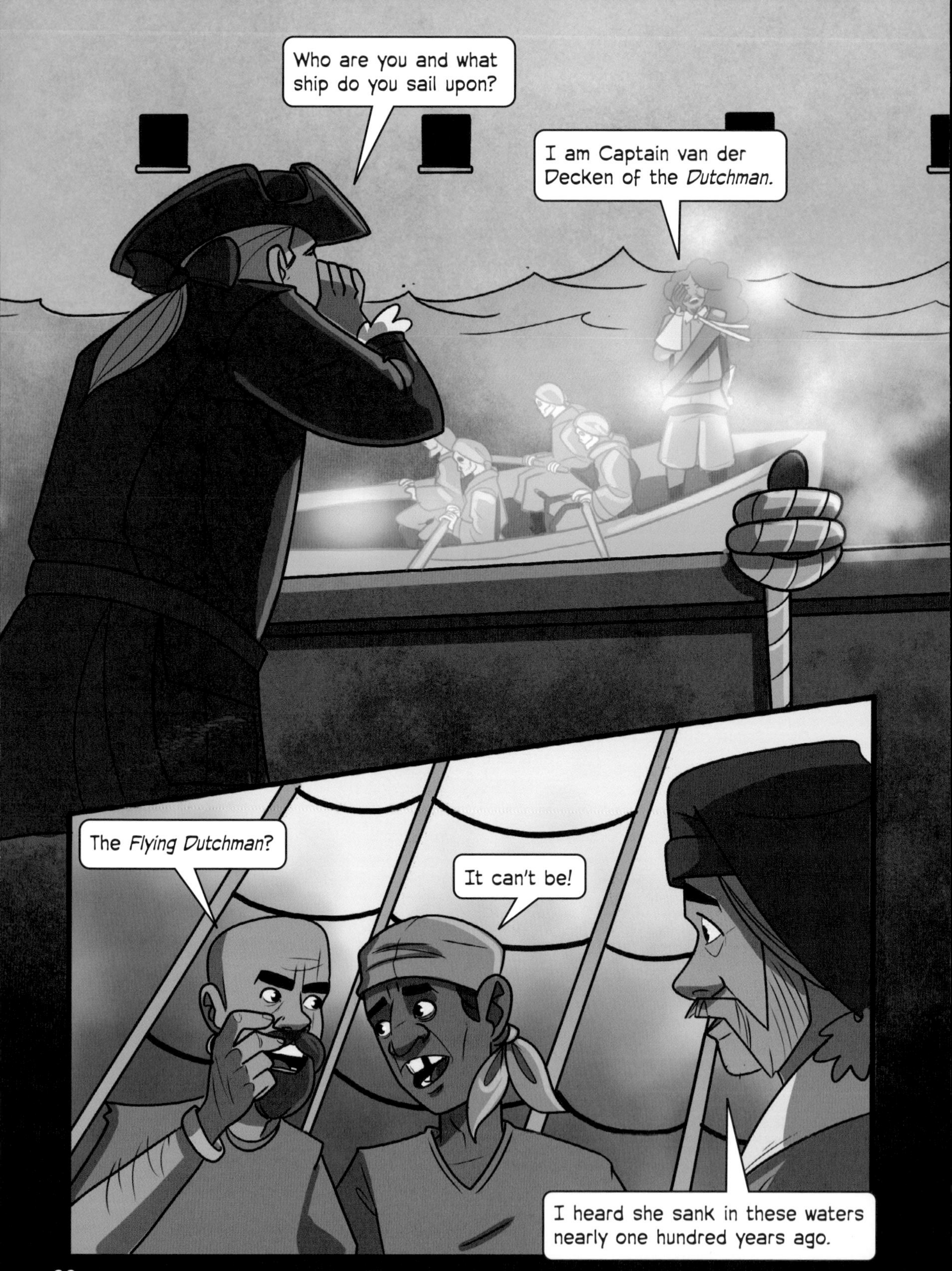
Who are you and what ship do you sail upon?
I am Captain van der Decken of the *Dutchman.*
The *Flying Dutchman*?
It can't be!
I heard she sank in these waters nearly one hundred years ago.

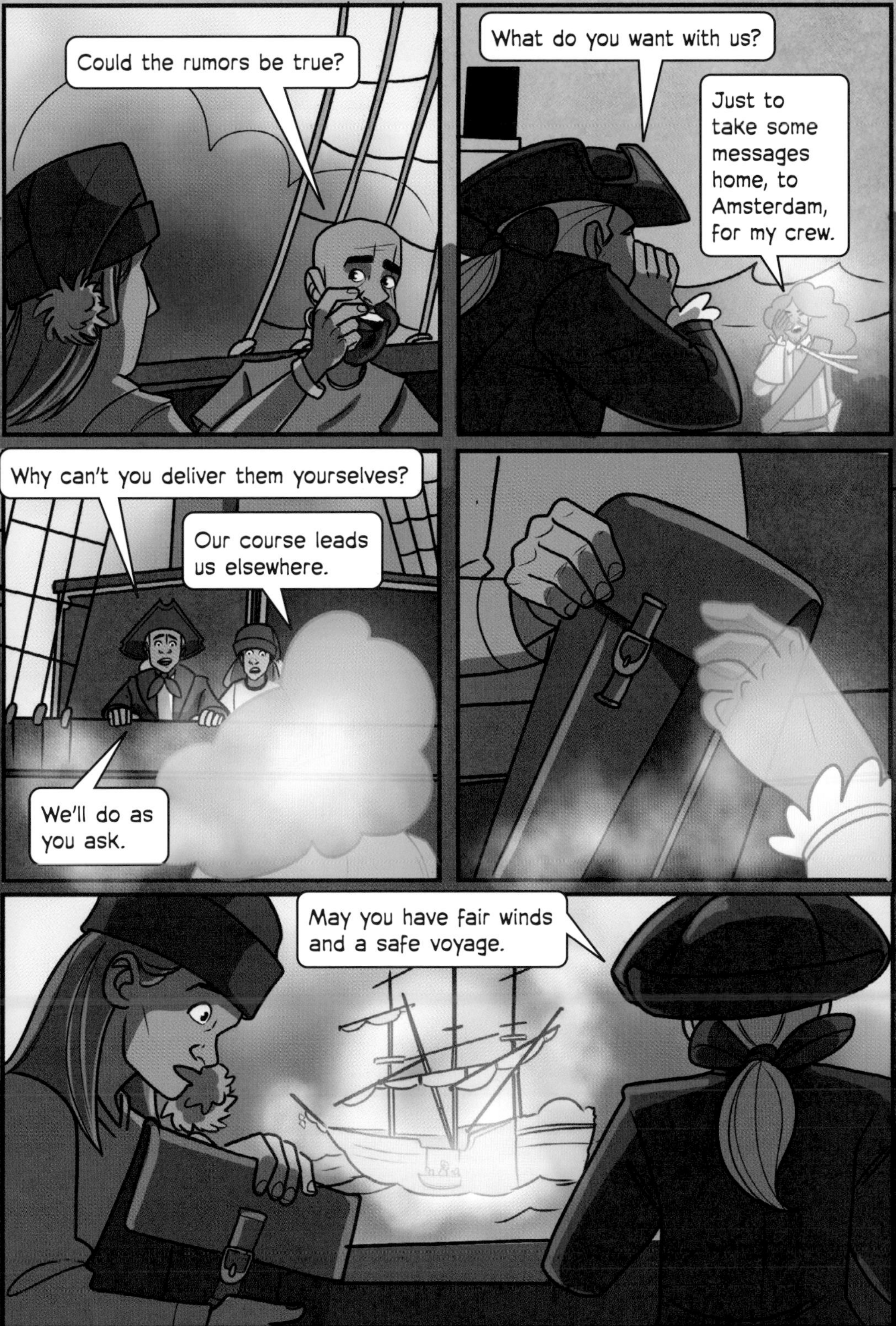
Could the rumors be true?
What do you want with us?
Just to take some messages home, to Amsterdam, for my crew.
Why can't you deliver them yourselves?
Our course leads us elsewhere.
We'll do as you ask.
May you have fair winds and a safe voyage.

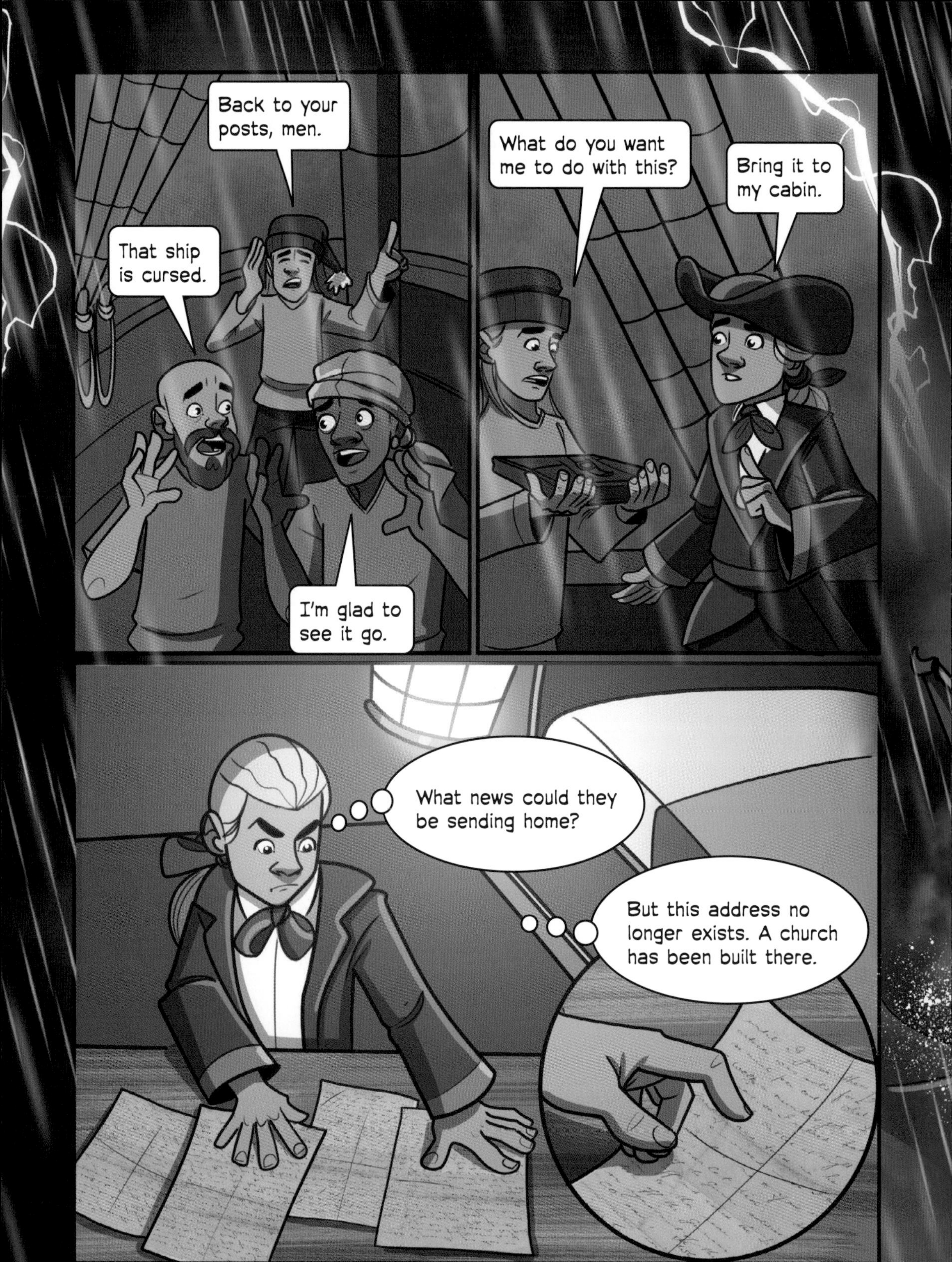

Back to your posts, men.
That ship is cursed.
I'm glad to see it go.
What do you want me to do with this?
Bring it to my cabin.
What news could they be sending home?
But this address no longer exists. A church has been built there.

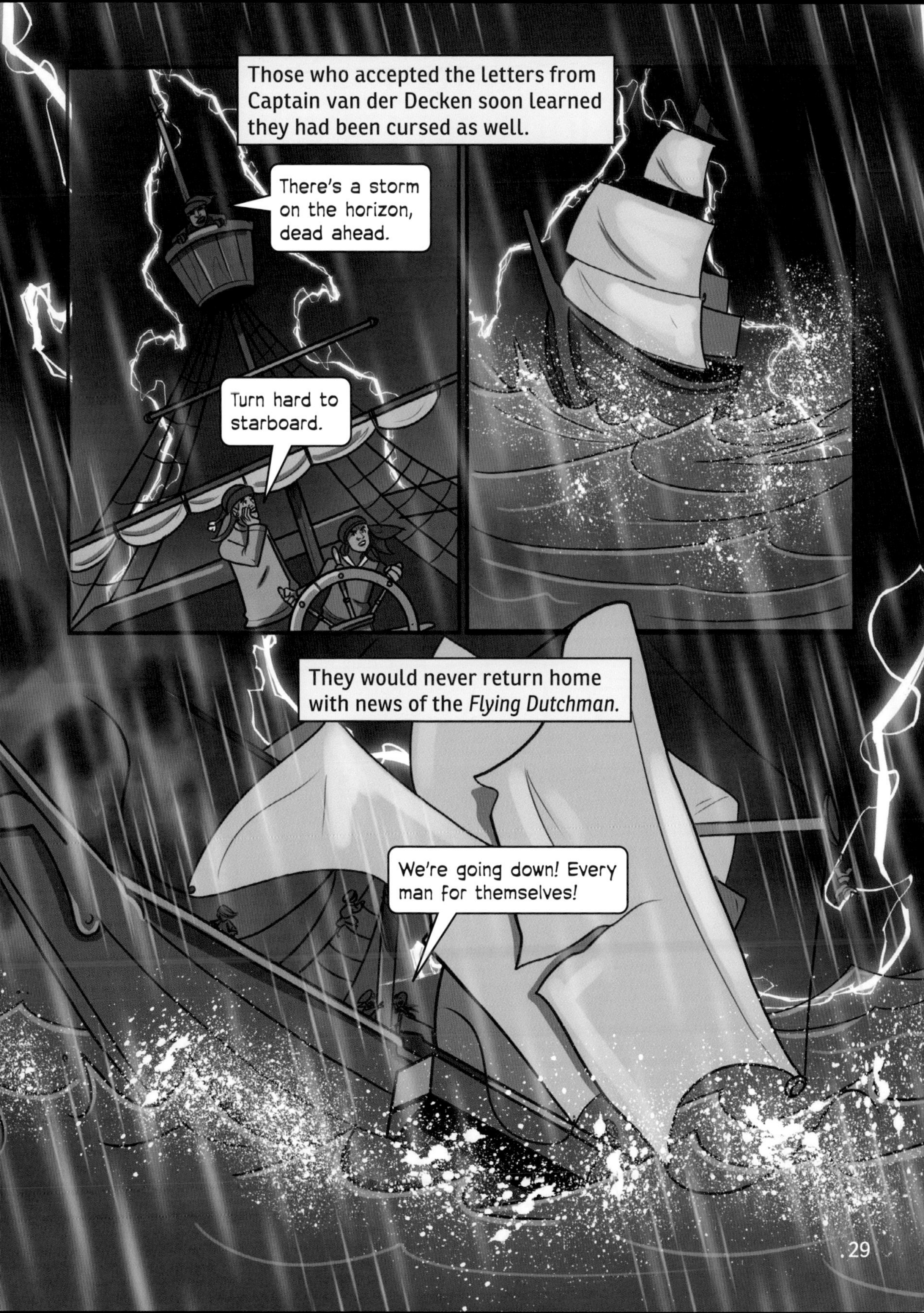
Those who accepted the letters from Captain van der Decken soon learned they had been cursed as well.
There's a storm on the horizon, dead ahead.
Turn hard to starboard.
They would never return home with news of the *Flying Dutchman*.
We're going down! Every man for themselves!

CHAPTER 4
FAMOUS SIGHTINGS

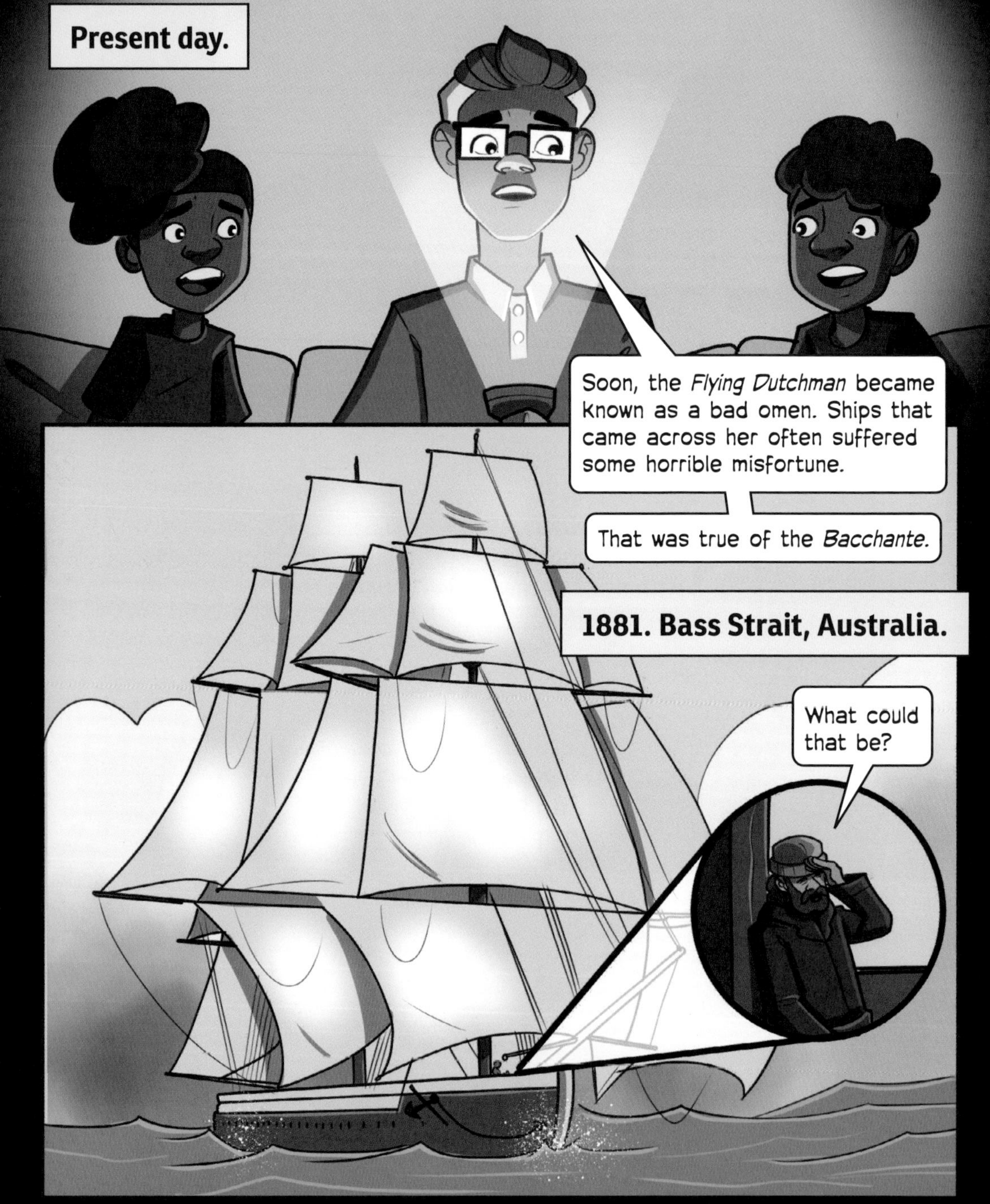
Present day.
Soon, the *Flying Dutchman* became known as a bad omen. Ships that came across her often suffered some horrible misfortune.
That was true of the *Bacchante*.
1881. Bass Strait, Australia.
What could that be?

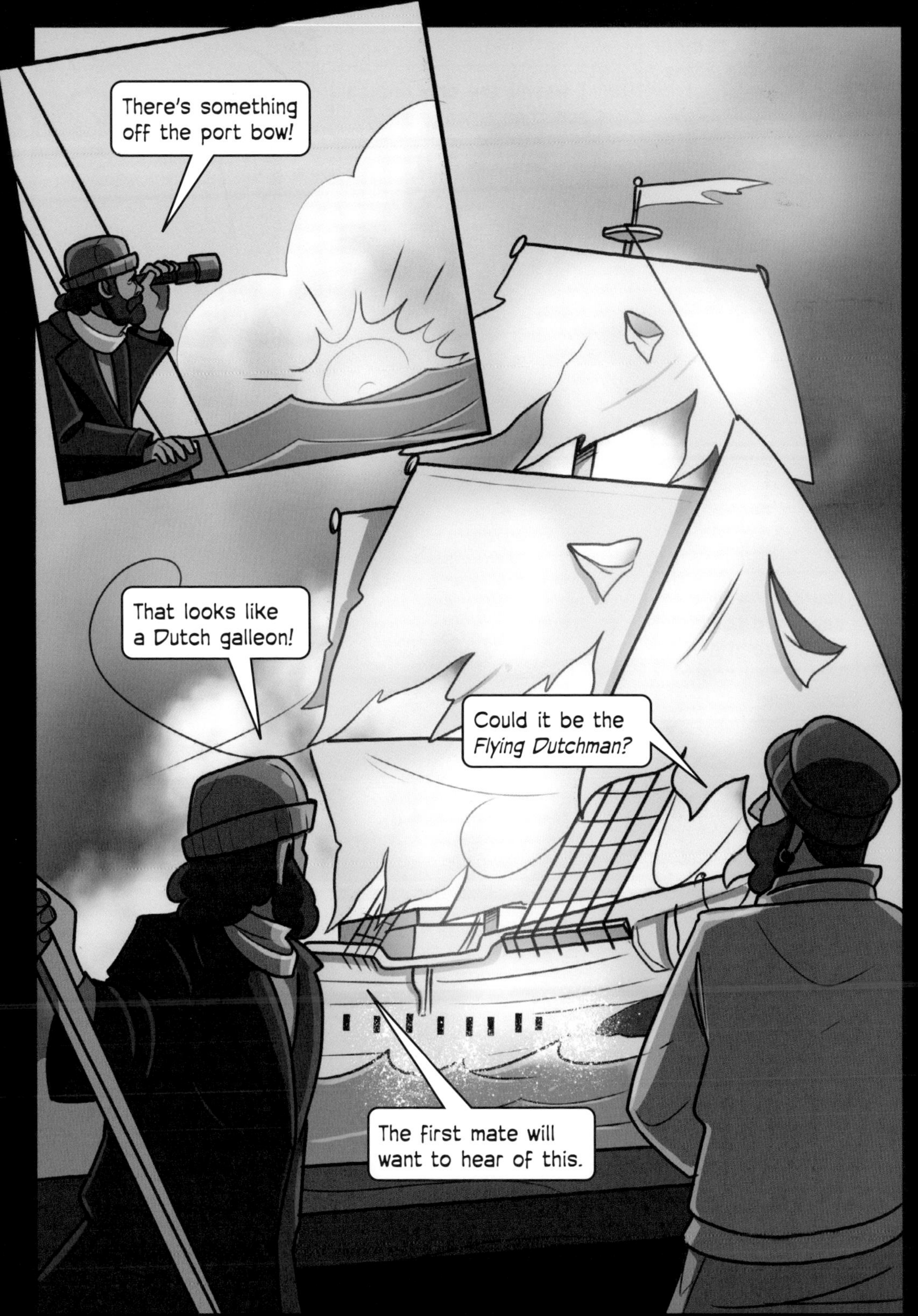
There's something off the port bow!
That looks like a Dutch galleon!
Could it be the *Flying Dutchman?*
The first mate will want to hear of this.

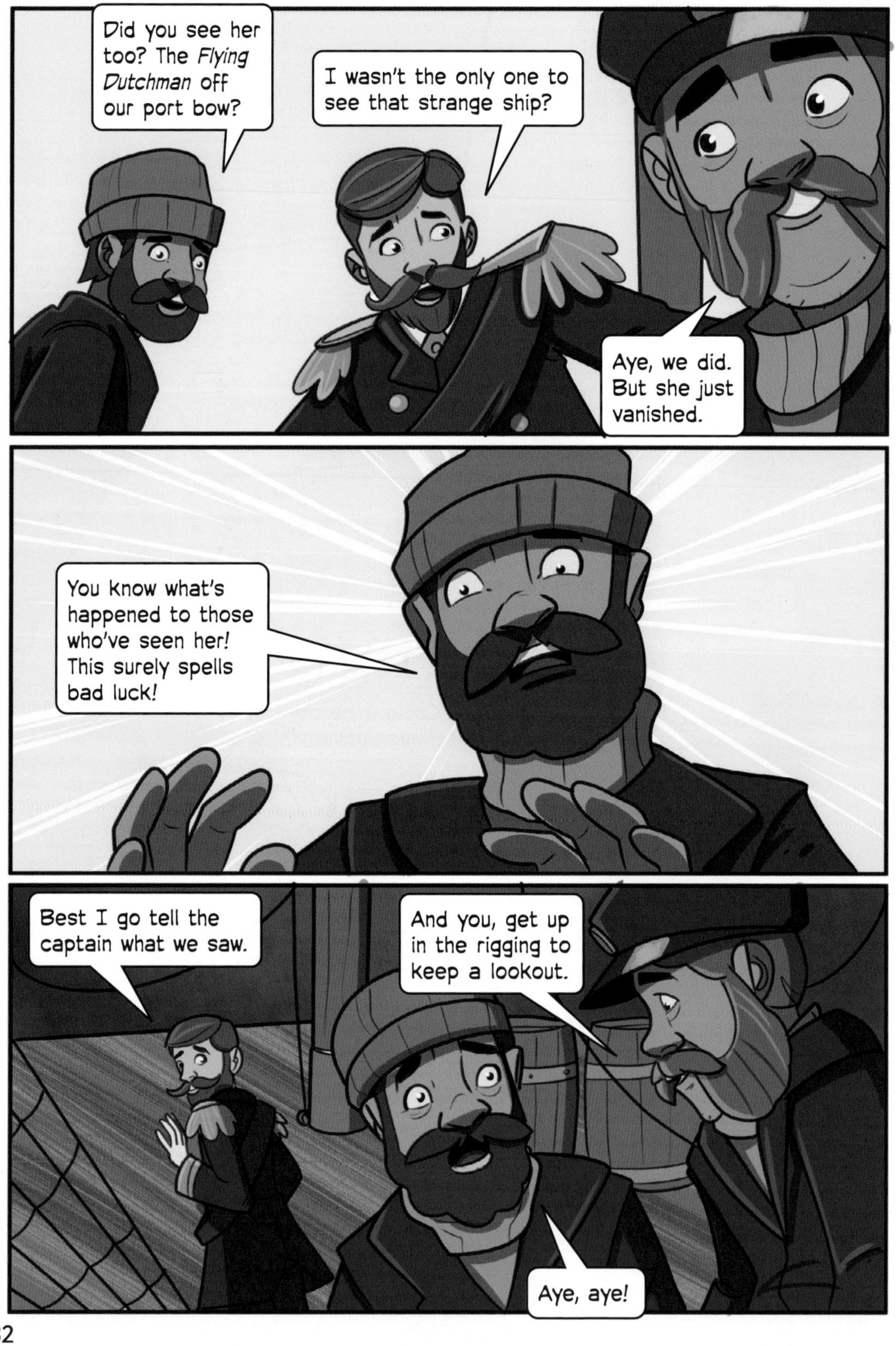
Did you see her too? The *Flying Dutchman* off our port bow?
I wasn't the only one to see that strange ship?
Aye, we did. But she just vanished.
You know what's happened to those who've seen her! This surely spells bad luck!
Best I go tell the captain what we saw.
And you, get up in the rigging to keep a lookout.
Aye, aye!

At some point that morning, the curse of the *Flying Dutchman* struck.

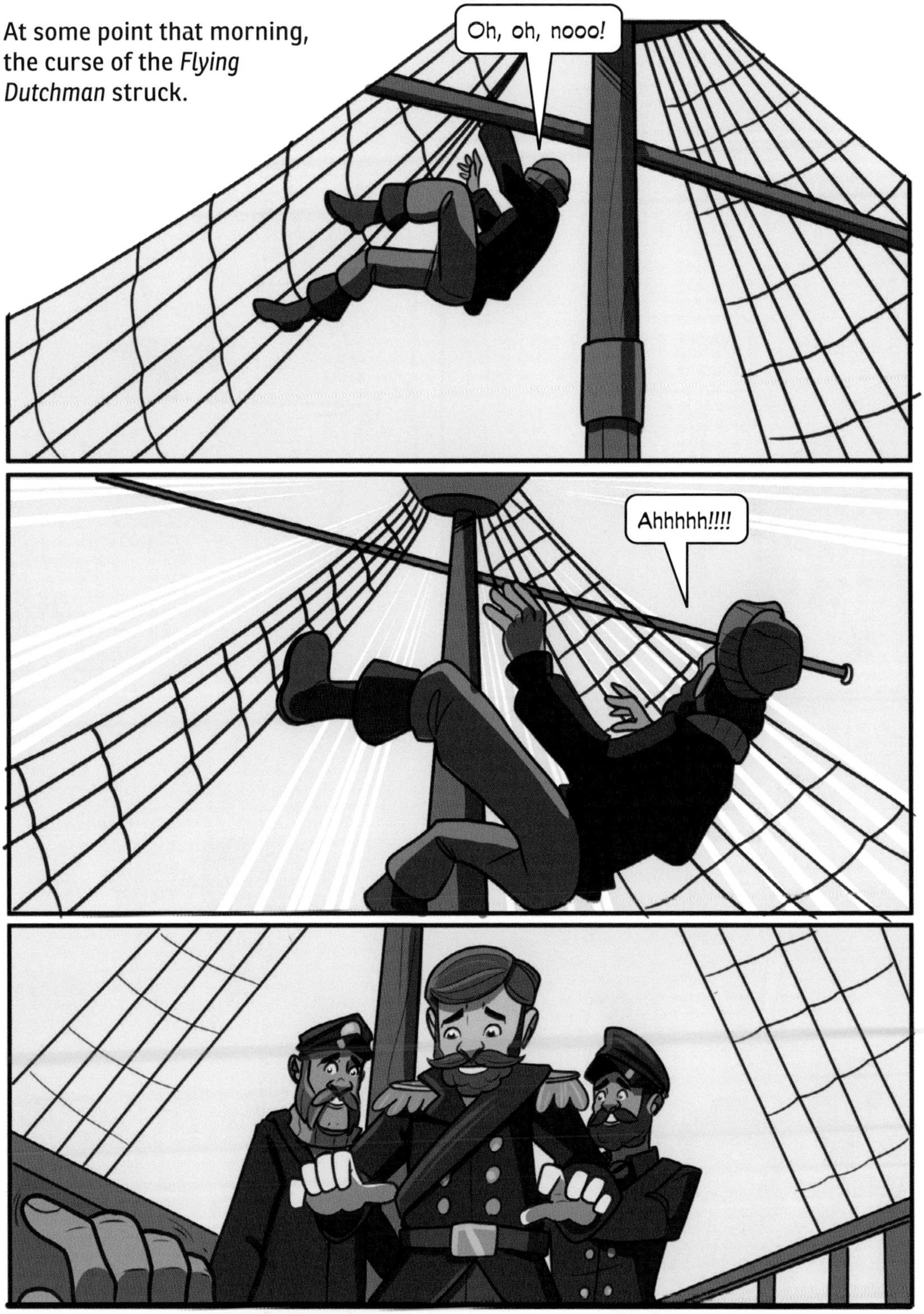

Oh, oh, nooo!
Ahhhhh!!!!

The sailor who first saw the ghost ship fell to his death.

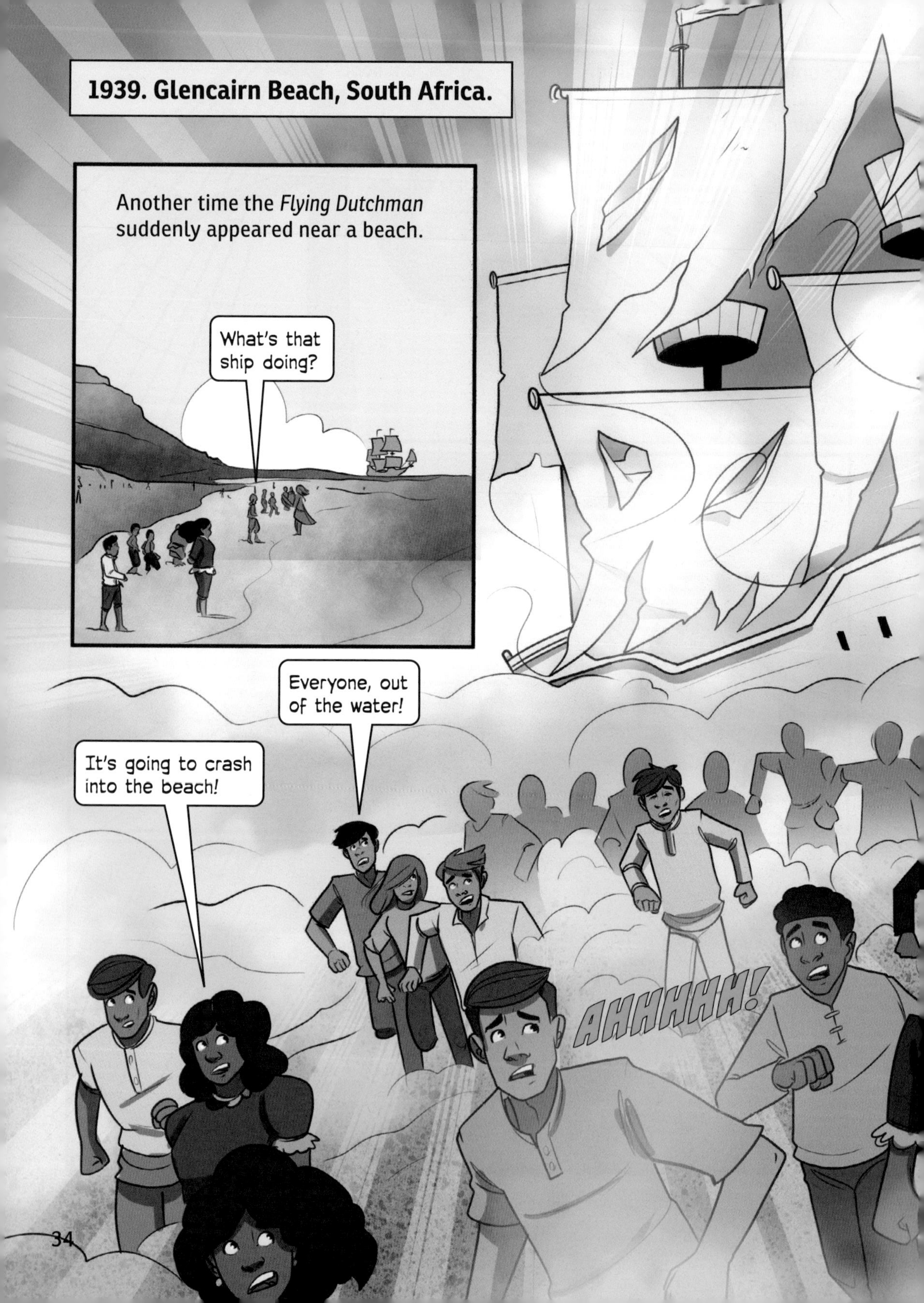
1939. Glencairn Beach, South Africa.
Another time the *Flying Dutchman* suddenly appeared near a beach.
What's that ship doing?
Everyone, out of the water!
It's going to crash into the beach!
AHHHHH!

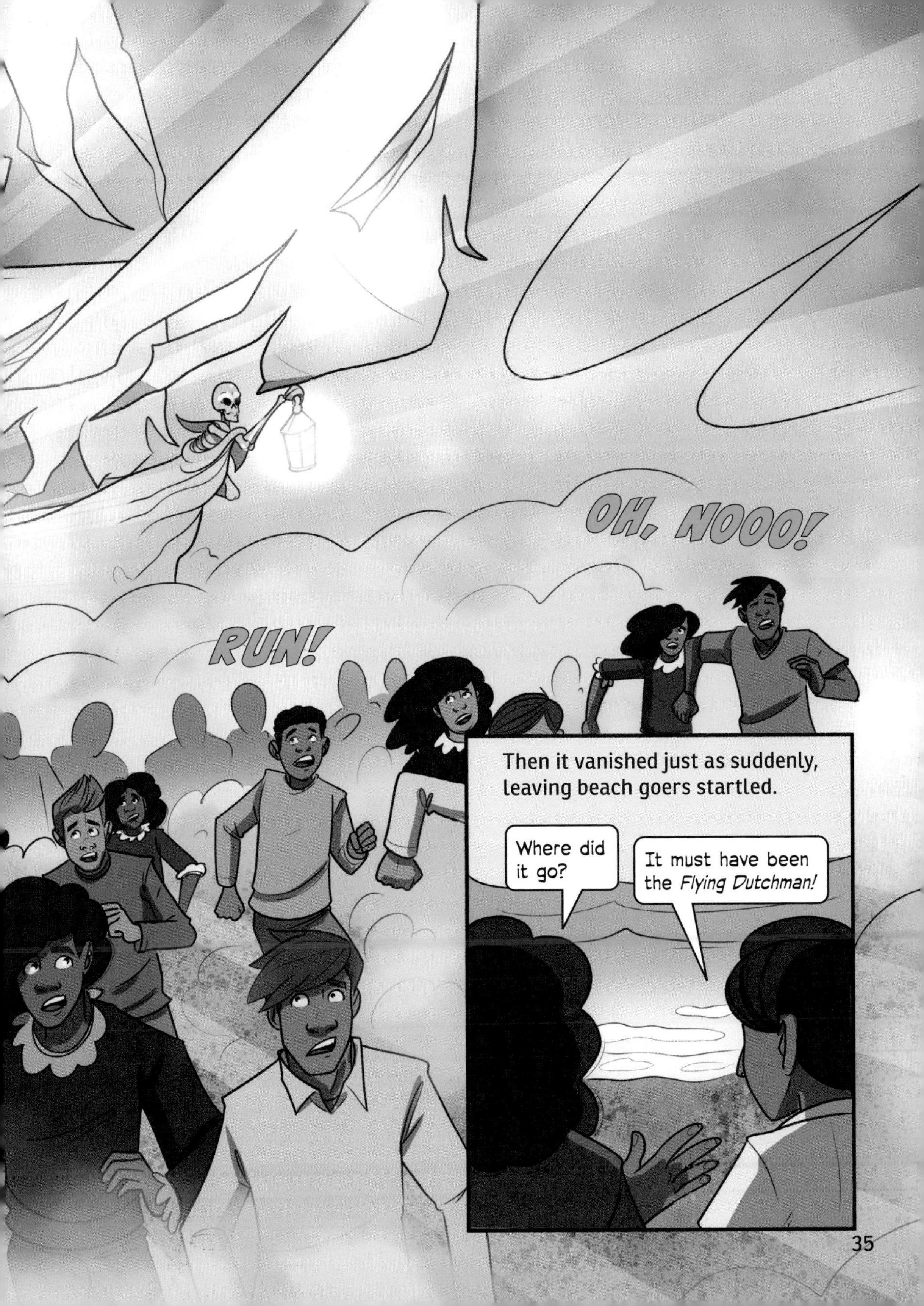
OH, NOOO!
RUN!
Then it vanished just as suddenly, leaving beach goers startled.
Where did it go?
It must have been the *Flying Dutchman!*

1945, Suez Canal.

And one of the most recently reported sightings of the *Flying Dutchman* occurred during World War II.

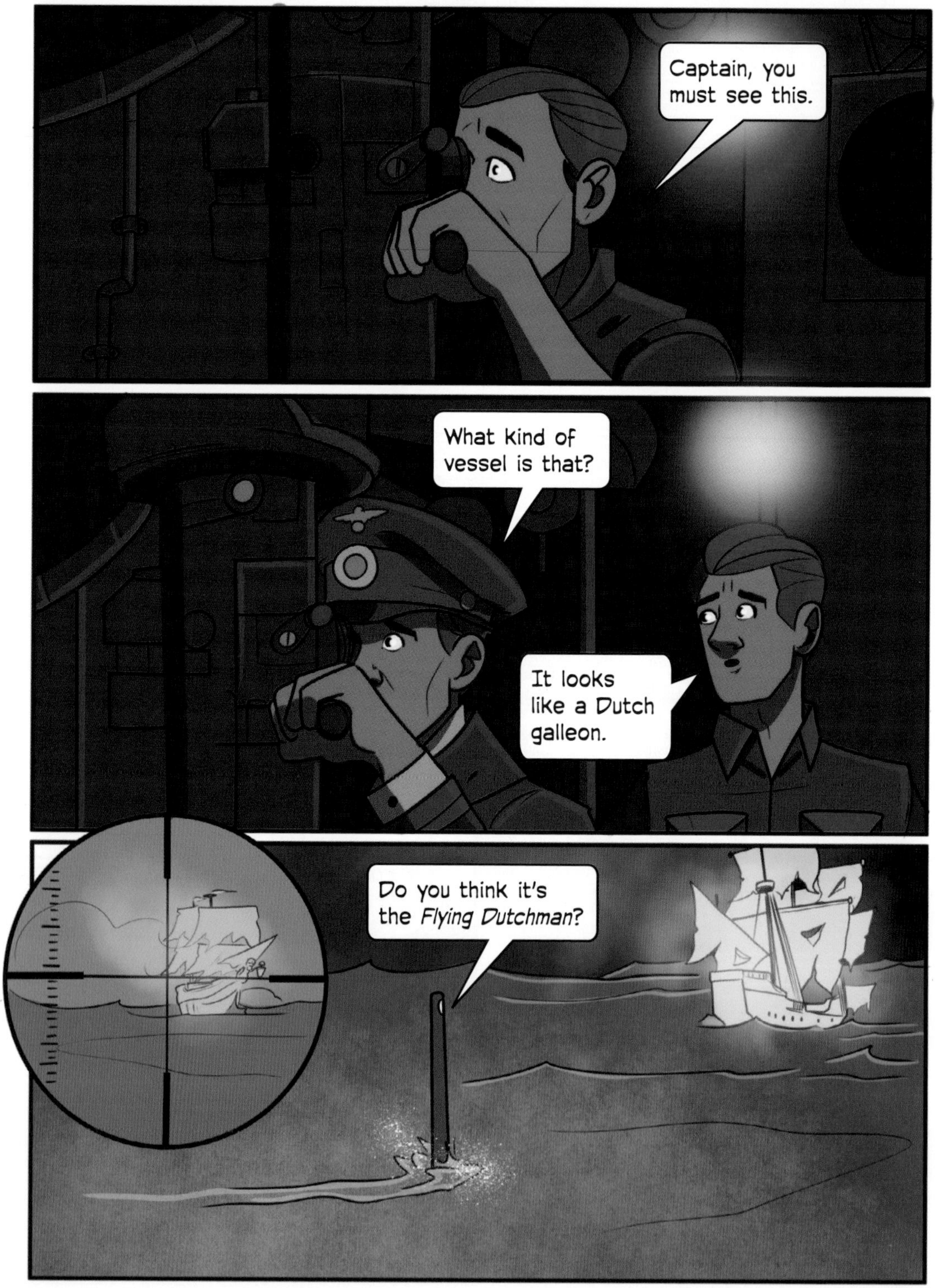
Captain, you must see this.
What kind of vessel is that?
It looks like a Dutch galleon.
Do you think it's the *Flying Dutchman*?

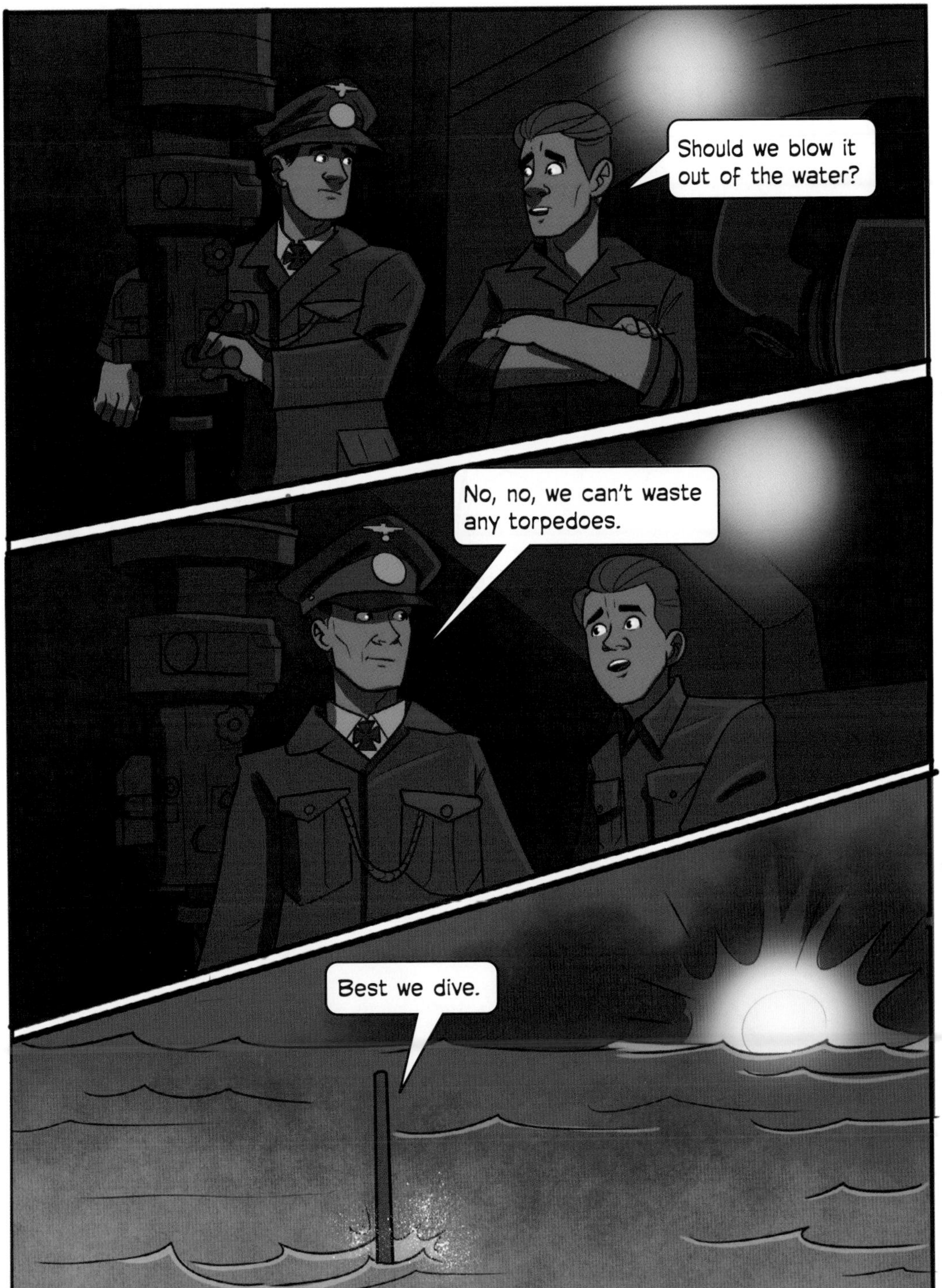
Should we blow it out of the water?
No, no, we can't waste any torpedoes.
Best we dive.

Whether the German U-boat survived its run-in with the *Flying Dutchman* is unknown.

CHAPTER 5
THE LEGEND LIVES ON

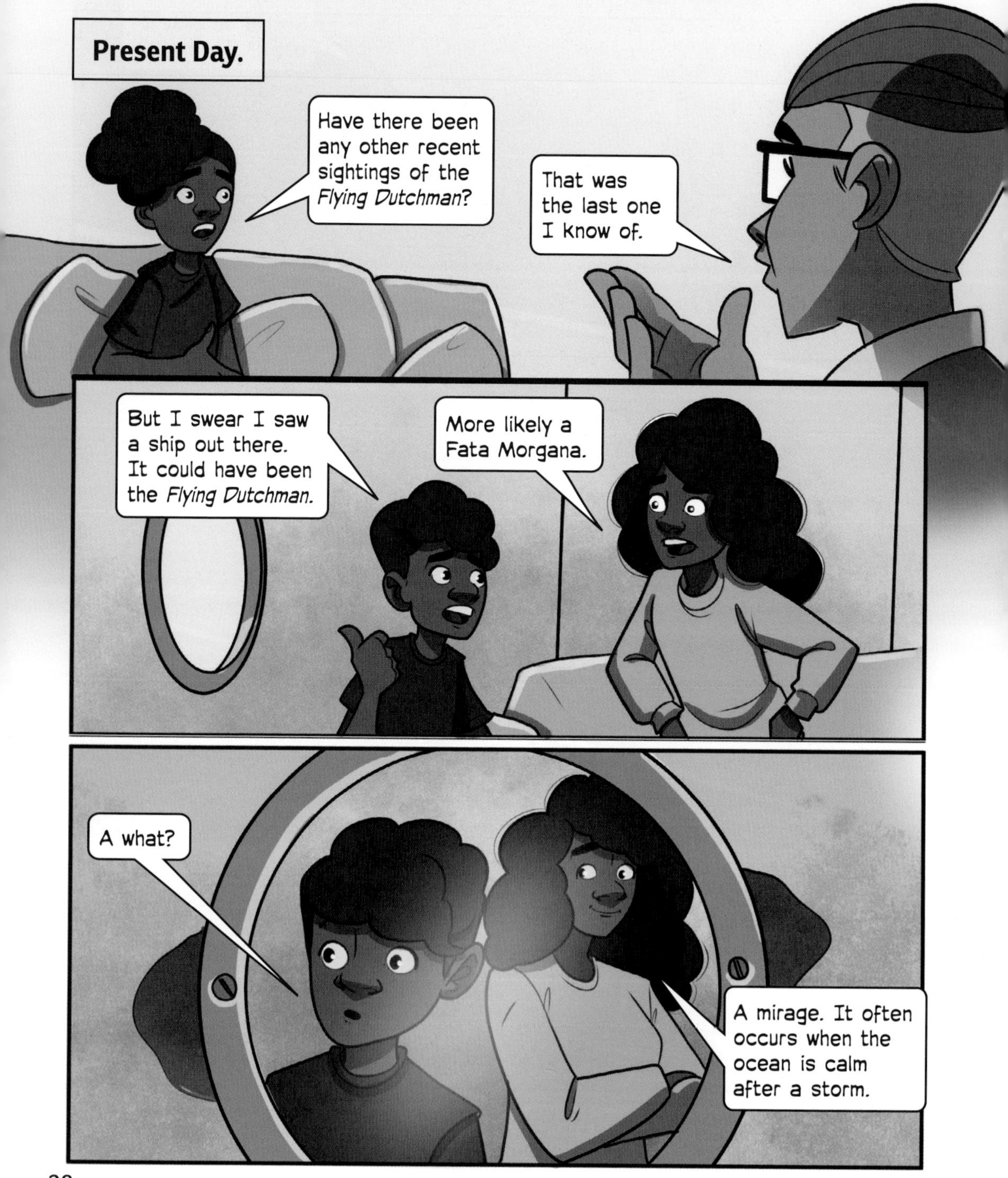
Present Day.
Have there been any other recent sightings of the *Flying Dutchman*?
That was the last one I know of.
But I swear I saw a ship out there. It could have been the *Flying Dutchman*.
More likely a Fata Morgana.
A what?
A mirage. It often occurs when the ocean is calm after a storm.

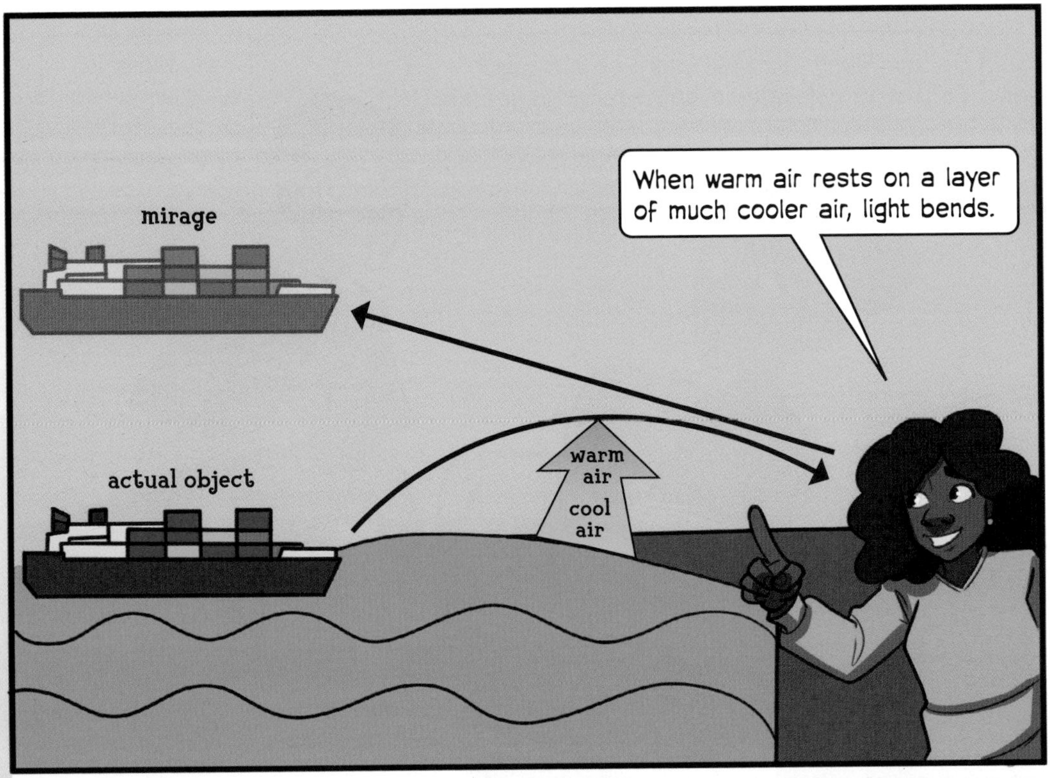
When warm air rests on a layer of much cooler air, light bends.
mirage
actual object
warm air
cool air

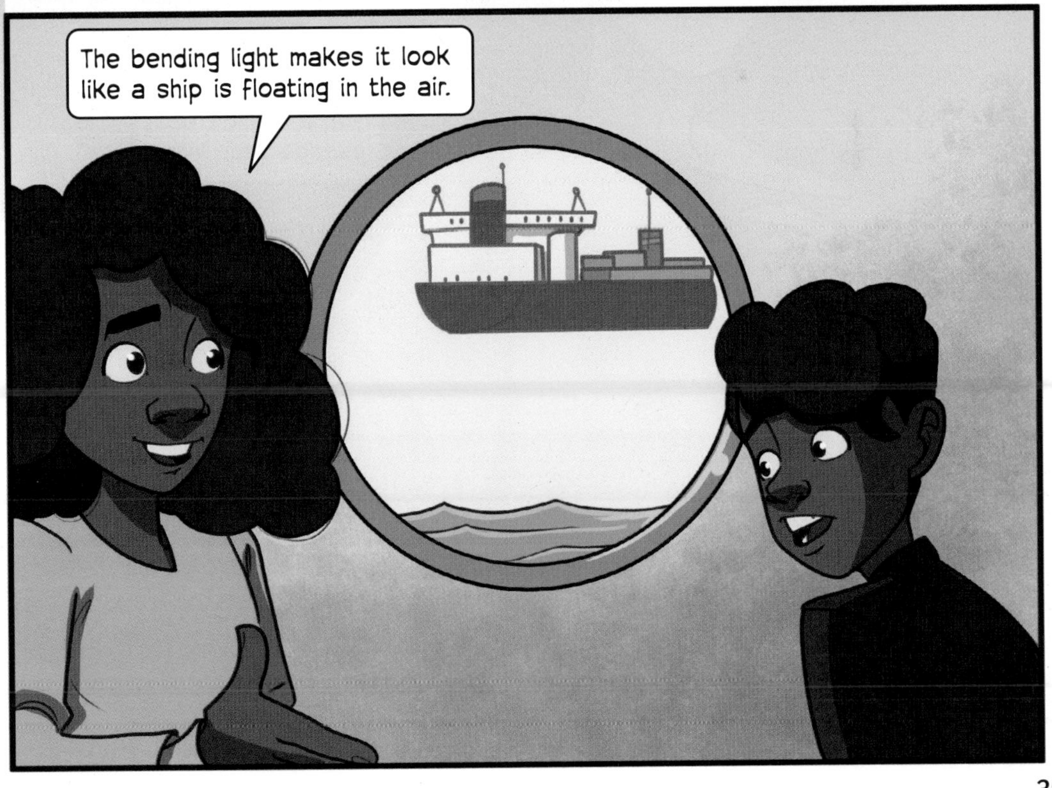
The bending light makes it look like a ship is floating in the air.

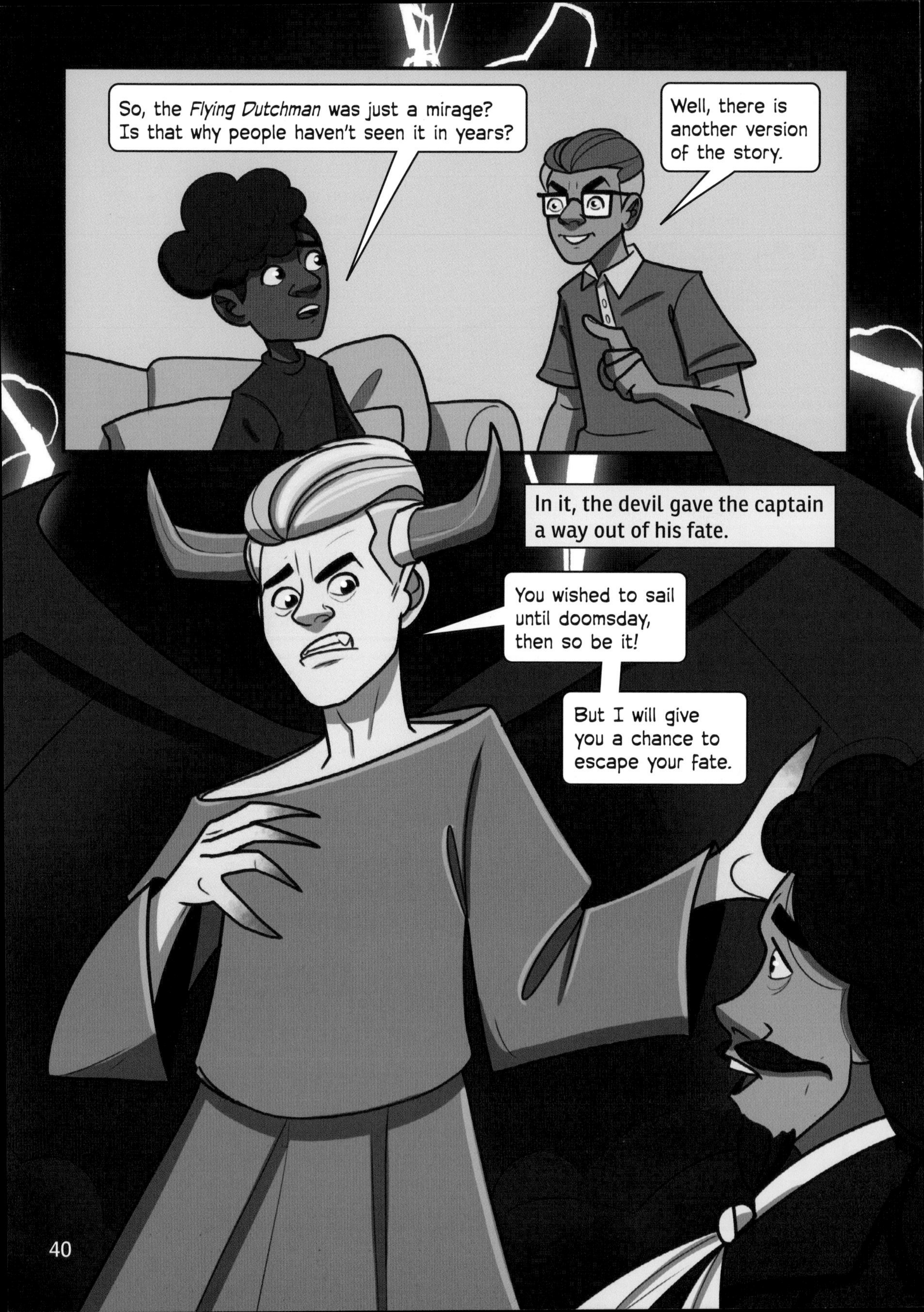

So, the *Flying Dutchman* was just a mirage? Is that why people haven't seen it in years?
Well, there is another version of the story.
In it, the devil gave the captain a way out of his fate.
You wished to sail until doomsday, then so be it!
But I will give you a chance to escape your fate.

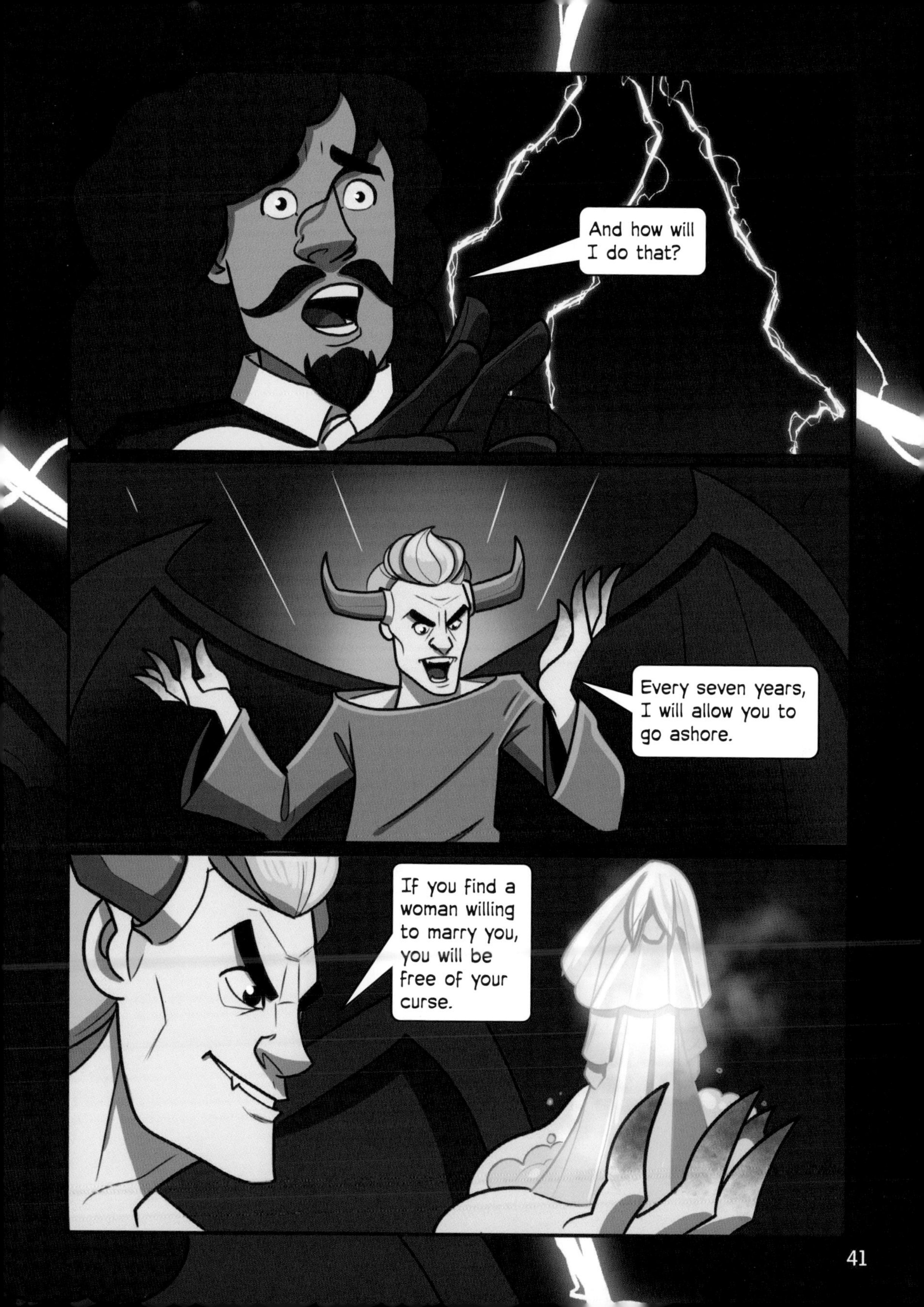
And how will I do that?
Every seven years, I will allow you to go ashore.
If you find a woman willing to marry you, you will be free of your curse.

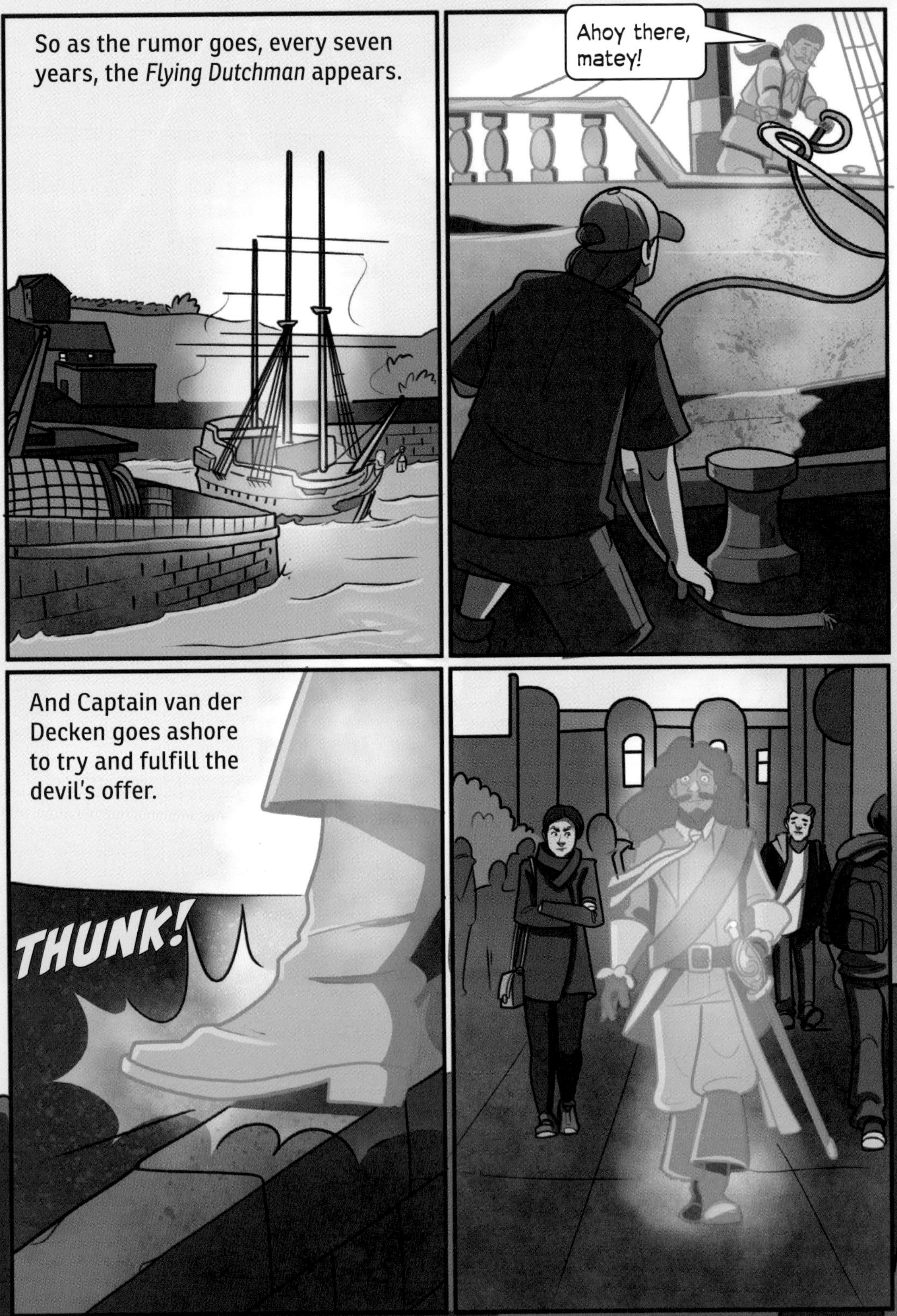
So as the rumor goes, every seven years, the *Flying Dutchman* appears.
Ahoy there, matey!
And Captain van der Decken goes ashore to try and fulfill the devil's offer.
THUNK!

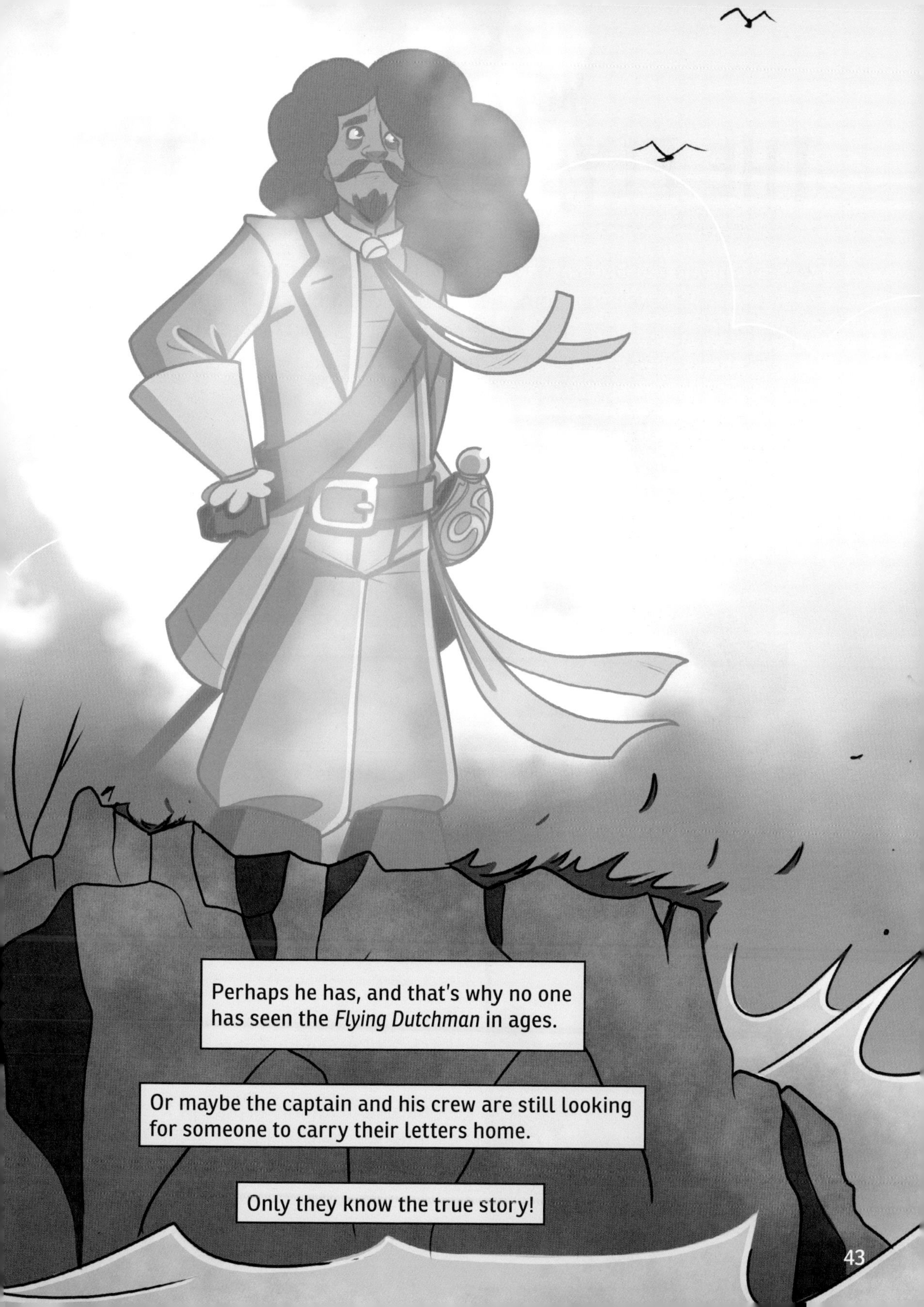
Perhaps he has, and that's why no one has seen the *Flying Dutchman* in ages.
Or maybe the captain and his crew are still looking for someone to carry their letters home.
Only they know the true story!

MORE ABOUT
THE FLYING DUTCHMAN

- Captain van der Decken was not the only sailor to inspire tales of the *Flying Dutchman*. Some people believed a different captain traded his soul to the devil so he could sail his ship faster. They think he is the source of the *Flying Dutchman* tales.

- The Fata Morgana is named after a witch. Some believed she used mirages to lure sailors to their deaths.

- The *Flying Dutchman* has appeared in numerous books and movies. One of the first mentions of the ghost ship was in two books from the 1790s. These early tales of the *Flying Dutchman* helped spread rumors of the ghost ship.

- During the 1881 sighting of the *Flying Dutchman*, Prince George of England was aboard the HMS *Bacchante*. In his report of the journey, he mentions seeing the ghost ship.

- The idea that the *Flying Dutchman*'s captain comes to shore every seven years was first mentioned in an opera from the 1800s.

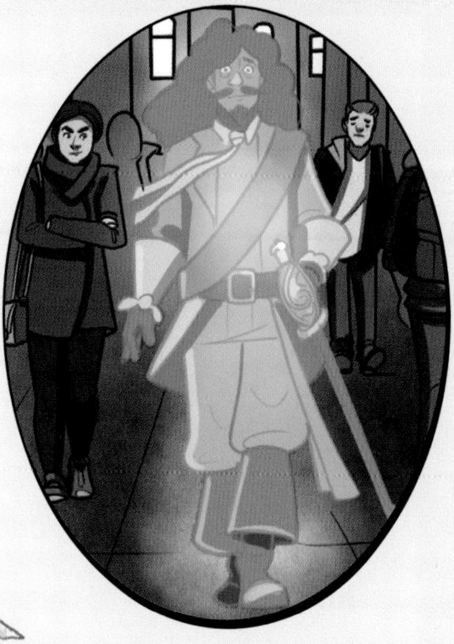

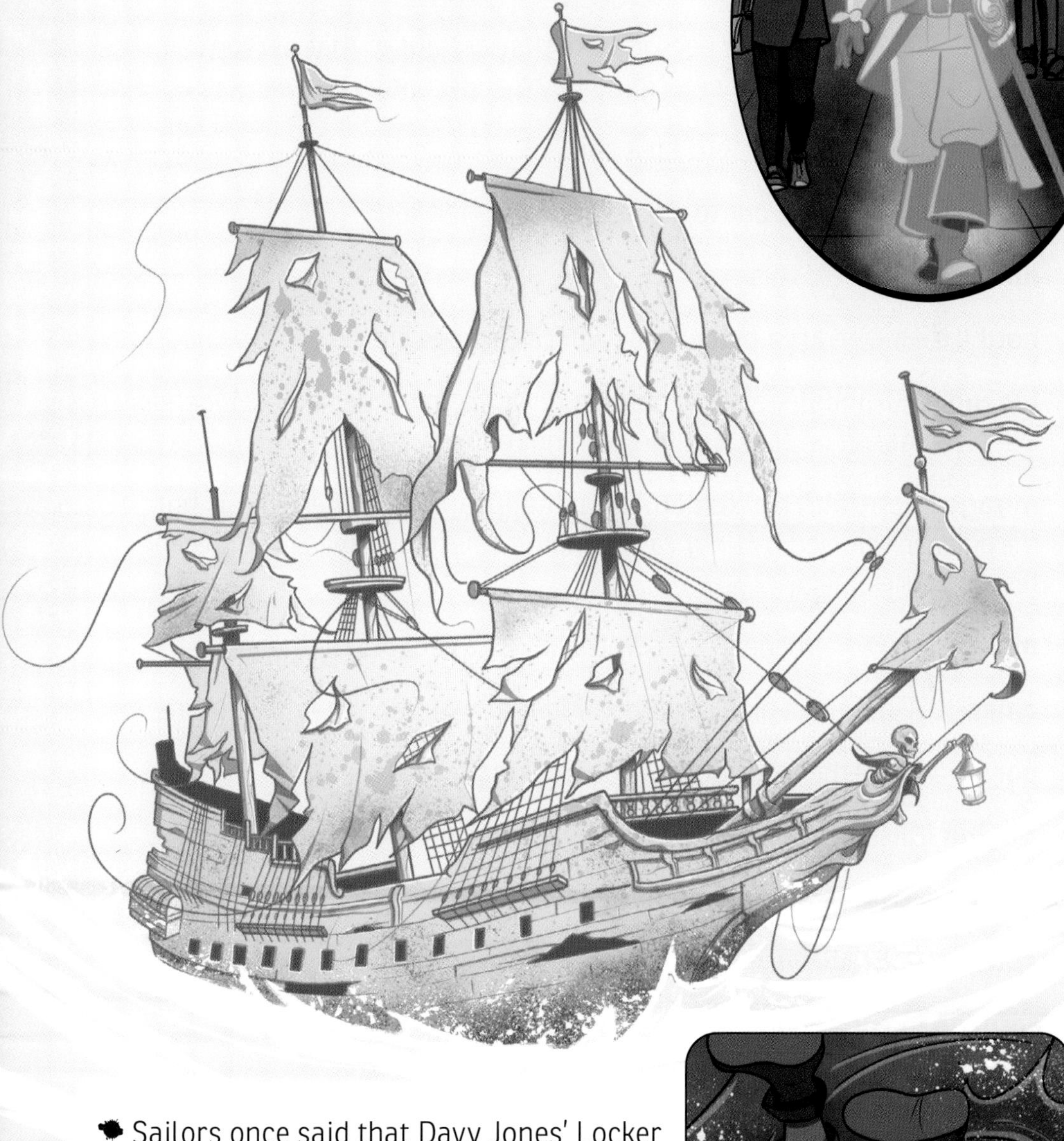

- Sailors once said that Davy Jones' Locker was the resting place for sailors who had died and been buried at sea.

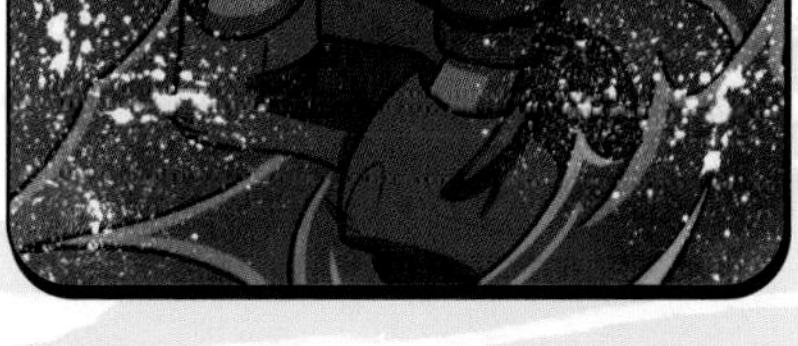

GLOSSARY

bow (BAU)—the front of a ship

cargo (KAHR-goh)—the goods carried by a ship, vehicle, or aircraft

fate (FAYT)—events in a person's life that are out of that person's control or are said to be determined by a supernatural power

furl (FURL)—to roll or fold up a sail

hail (HAYL)—to call out to get someone's attention

hoist (HOIST)—to raise

hold (HOHLD)—area below deck where cargo is stored

legend (LEJ-uhnd)—a story handed down from earlier times; legends are often based on fact, but they are not entirely true

mirage (muh-RAZH)—something that appears to be there but is not; mirages are caused by light rays bending where air layers of different temperatures meet

mutiny (MYOOT-uh-nee)—a revolt against the captain of a ship

omen (OH-men)—a sign of something that will happen in the future

port (PORT)—the left side of a ship looking forward

rigging (RIHG-ing)—the ropes, chains, and cables on a ship's mast

route (ROUT)—the path you follow to get somewhere

starboard (STAR-burd)—the right side of a ship looking forward

torpedo (tor-PEE-doh)—an underwater missile

READ MORE

Gagne, Tammy. *Haunted Ships.* North Mankato, MN: Capstone Press, 2018.

Peterson, Megan Cooley. *The Flying Dutchman: The Doomed Ghost Ship.* North Mankato, MN: Capstone Press, 2020.

Polinsky, Paige V. *Ghost Ships.* Minneapolis, Bellwether Media, Inc. 2020.

INTERNET SITES

All That's Interesting: The Mystery of the Flying Dutchman Explained by the Physics of Light
allthatsinteresting.com/flying-dutchman

History Collection—The Truth Behind the Legends of the Flying Dutchman
historycollection.com/the-truth-behind-the-legends-of-the-flying-dutchman/2

SKYbrary—Fata Morgana
skybrary.aero/articles/fata-morgana

ABOUT THE AUTHOR

Photo by Russell Griesmer

Blake A. Hoena grew up in central Wisconsin, where he wrote stories about robots conquering the moon and trolls lumbering around the woods behind his parents' house. He now lives in Minnesota and enjoys writing about fun things like history, space aliens, cryptids, and superheroes. Blake has written more than 50 chapter books and dozens of graphic novels for children.

ABOUT THE ILLUSTRATOR

Photo by Emma Brown

Alan Brown is a freelance illustrator who has created artwork for Disney, Warner Bros., and the BBC, while continuing to provide illustrations for children's books and comics. Alan has worked mainly on children's books for kids who find it hard to engage and be enthusiastic about reading. These clients include Harper Collins, Capstone, Ransom, Franklin Watts, and Ben 10 Omniverse.